Handbook for Planning an Effective Literature Program

Kindergarten Through Grade Twelve

Prepared Under the Direction of the
Language Arts and Foreign Languages Unit
Curriculum, Instruction, and Assessment Division
California State Department of Education

Publishing Information

The *Handbook for Planning an Effective Literature Program* was developed by the Literature Handbook Committee, working in cooperation with George Nemetz and Leonard Hull, consultants, Language Arts and Foreign Languages Unit, California State Department of Education. (See the Acknowledgments for a list of committee members.) The final version of the publication was written by William Boly. The *Handbook* was edited by Theodore R. Smith, working in cooperation with George Nemetz and assisted by Janet Lundin, and prepared for photo-offset production by the staff of the Bureau of Publications. Cheryl Shawver McDonald created and prepared the interior design and illustrated the document. Paul Lee designed and prepared the cover. Typesetting was done by Anna Boyd and Lea Shimabukuro.

The document was published by the California State Department of Education, 721 Capitol Mall, Sacramento, California (mailing address: P.O. Box 944272, Sacramento, CA 94244-2720). It was printed by the Office of State Printing and distributed under the provisions of the Library Distribution Act and *Government Code* Section 11096.

Copies of this publication are available for $3 each, plus sales tax for California residents, from Publications Sales, California State Department of Education, P.O. Box 271, Sacramento, CA 95802-0271.

A list of other publications available from the Department may be found on page 63, or a complete list may be obtained by writing to the address above or by calling the sales unit in the Bureau of Publications: (916) 445-1260.

ISBN 0-8011-0320-7

Contents

Foreword

From the time they enter kindergarten until they graduate from high school, our students should find a high standard of thought and feeling at the heart of their English language arts education: great literature. I am convinced that transforming this prescription into a day-to-day reality for students in California's classrooms is one of the truly crucial tasks facing the public school reform movement. It is crucial because, according to American critic and writer, Alan Tate, ". . . the high forms of literature offer us the only complete, and thus the most responsible, versions of our experience."[1] Every child deserves a chance to explore this vast and challenging storehouse of socially empowering insights and ideas.

Following the passage of a legislatively mandated reform agenda in 1983, the schools have begun taking great strides in improving their literature programs. Figures from the California Basic Educational Data System indicate increasing enrollments in these programs. From 1982 to 1986 the number of students in grades nine through twelve increased by 5 percent; however, the number of students taking all categories of literature classes increased by 30 percent, and the number taking American literature classes increased by 55 percent.

Still, a great deal of work remains to be done. Literature is the key to a successful English program for all students, not just the academic elite; and for all educational levels, not just the high school years. Teaching literature well requires a formidable degree of learning, imagination, and energy. This handbook was prepared to provide practical advice to school-level planners, teachers, and parents as to how they can improve their school's literature program.

What are the hallmarks of an effective literature program? What can teachers do to bring the great works of literature—fiction and nonfiction, classic and contemporary, drama and poetry—to life? How can parents help? Answers to these and other key questions based on the latest research and the collective experience of a distinguished panel of educators are provided here. I salute those individuals who contributed their time and ideas to the preparation of this handbook, and I heartily recommend it to all those seeking to develop excellence in the teaching of literature. As a resource to your own creative thinking, may this handbook serve you well.

Bill Honig

SUPERINTENDENT OF PUBLIC INSTRUCTION

Preface

This handbook joins others that we have published in recent years in five curriculum areas: reading, writing, foreign languages, science, and mathematics. While these handbooks can be useful to all who wish to review and improve educational programs, they are particularly designed for those who plan and implement curricula at the school site level. In addition to classroom teachers, such groups might include school administrators, curriculum specialists, special consultants, parents, and students. The first purpose of these handbooks is to help such groups become fully aware of what constitutes excellence in a particular curricular area in the light of the most current findings of research regarding both content and appropriate teaching methods. Another purpose is to help such groups identify the strengths and weaknesses in existing programs and to select strategies for change when it is appropriate.

The checklist in this document is intended to facilitate the assessment of an existing program for the teaching of literature. If, as a result of such a review, it becomes apparent that changes need to be made in a program, the raters may wish to consult some of the publications listed in the "Selected References" of this document.

The group of California educators who served on the advisory committee that worked on this handbook and staff members of this agency who were assigned to the effort quickly discovered that the field of literature is not as process-oriented as other facets of the English–language arts curriculum, such as writing and reading, and that the publishing of a practical and useful handbook in literature would be more elusive and difficult to achieve. They did achieve their objective, however, and we are most grateful to the members of the advisory committee who worked on the document so hard and so long, to the contributing consultants who were asked to assist with difficult portions of the manuscript, to the many reactors who reviewed early drafts, and to staff members of this agency, consultants Leonard Hull and George Nemetz, who coordinated the entire effort.

In the *Handbook for Planning an Effective Literature Program,* literature is central to the curriculum in general and to the English language arts program in particular. We commend it to you and solicit support for our efforts to disseminate broadly its theme: Literature should be an essential subject for study by all students.

JAMES R. SMITH
DEPUTY SUPERINTENDENT FOR
CURRICULUM AND INSTRUCTIONAL
LEADERSHIP

FRANCIE ALEXANDER
DIRECTOR, CURRICULUM, INSTRUCTION,
AND ASSESSMENT DIVISION

TOMAS LOPEZ
MANAGER, OFFICE OF HUMANITIES AND
CURRICULUM SERVICES

Acknowledgments

The distinguished group of educators who served on the advisory committee for the preparation of this handbook worked long and hard at the task. Through no fault of their own, the undertaking was subjected to several frustrating delays. The fact that it is finally being published is a tribute to the patience and persistence of these educators and to the depth of knowledge they brought to the task. Superintendent of Public Instruction Bill Honig and his immediate staff are most grateful for this important contribution to ongoing efforts to improve the teaching of literature in California. They congratulate the members of the advisory committee, other educators who served as reactors to earlier drafts of the manuscript, and staff members George F. Nemetz and Leonard Hull, who served as consultants to the committee and coordinators of the undertaking.

The following were the members of the advisory committee:

Jacqueline L. Chaparro, Coordinator, North Inland Educational Services, Office of the San Diego County Superintendent of Schools

William J. Fairgrieve, Teacher, English Department, Lodi High School

Thomas Gage, English Department, Humboldt State University, Arcata

Walter Loban, Professor Emeritus, University of California, Berkeley

Denise Nessel, Independent Reading–Language Arts Consultant, San Francisco

Shirley Patch, Teacher, Del Paso Manor Elementary School, San Juan Unified School District, Sacramento

Virginia M. Reid, Retired, former President, National Council of Teachers of English; and former Consultant in Reading, Oakland Unified School District

Hugh Richmond, English Department, University of California, Berkeley

Leo Ruth, Supervisor of Teacher Education, University of California, Berkeley

John Oliver Simon, Former Executive Director, California Poets in the Schools; and Bilingual Classroom Teacher, Oakland Unified School District

William Thomas, Curriculum Specialist, Mt. Diablo Unified School District, Concord

Ariel Tomioka, California Poets in the Schools, Carmichael

Norma Willson, Language Arts Consultant, Torrance Unified School District

Yolanda Garfias Woo, Reading Resource Teacher, Compensatory Education Office, Lafayette School, San Francisco Unified School District

Barbara Zussman, Teacher, English Department, Beverly Hills High School

The principal writer of the *Handbook* was **William Boly** from Portland, Oregon.

The compiler of the committee's deliberations was **Robert Beck** from Berkeley.

The following consultants from the California State Department of Education provided staff support:

Beth Breneman, Consultant, California Assessment Program
Catharine Farrell, Zellerbach Family Fund Consultant attached to the Language Arts and Foreign Languages Unit
Mae Gundlach, Consultant, Language Arts and Foreign Languages Unit
M. Bruce Hagen, Consultant, Staff Development Unit
Shirley Hazlett, Consultant, Language Arts and Foreign Languages Unit
Tirso Serrano, Consultant, Health, Nutrition, and Physical Education Unit

Other major contributors to this publication were:

Janis R. Cox. Coordinator, Kindergarten Through Grade Twelve Curriculum and Faculty Development, Office of the President, University of California
Phil Daro, Executive Director, California Mathematics Project, Office of the President, University of California
Ed Farrell, Professor of Education, University of Texas, Austin
Karen Nemetz, Principal, Mission Avenue Elementary School, Carmichael
James Squire, Executive Consultant, Senior Vice-President, retired, Silver, Burdett & Ginn, Inc.; and former Executive Secretary, National Council of Teachers of English

We also wish to thank **Harry McPherson,** the husband of Jessamyn West and former Superintendent, Office of the Napa County Superintendent of Schools, who provided the material for Jessamyn West on page 25.

In Memoriam

Robert W. Horan, San Lorenzo, author of the first draft of the manuscript
Jackson Burgess, English Department, University of California, Berkeley, member of the advisory committee

---

The Committee developed this mandala or graphic symbol of the universe as a way of depicting the efficacy of an exemplary literature program.

Literature evokes students' emotional and intellectual response, which they are motivated to share with others and possibly to modify as they grow in their understanding of a work.

Literature heightens students' sensitivities and deepens critical thought.

Literature serves as a pleasurable, effective basis for reading instruction and encourages independent reading.

Literature conveys the recorded experience of the human condition, enabling individuals to transcend time, place, age, individual condition, and culture.

Literature introduces students to the cultures of the world and helps them become culturally literate in American society.

Introduction and Overview

The study of the great works of literature is the core of the English–language arts program. Unfortunately, for a variety of reasons, the study of literature has been neglected in recent times. In the 1970s, for example, a dominant trend in many California high schools was the relaxation of academic standards for the majority of students. "The proportion of students taking a general program of study has increased from 12 percent in 1964 to 42 percent in 1979."[1] This trend meant that such course titles as "Mass Media," "Mystery and Detective Stories," and "Sports Fiction" were taking the place of Shakespeare, Dostoyevsky, the Bronte sisters, and Robert Frost in the mainstream curriculum. Meanwhile, in the elementary schools, rote learning had taken hold. A survey of classroom practice in elementary schools found that up to 70 percent of the time allocated for reading instruction (about an hour a day) was being spent on "seatwork"—filling-in-the-blanks and circling or underlining answers on mind-numbing "skill sheets."[2] According to a report of the National Commission on Reading, "In the course of a school year, it would not be uncommon for a child in the elementary grades to bring home 1,000 workbook pages and skill sheets completed during a reading period."[3]

Unfortunately, little evidence indicates that this paper blizzard was achieving the desired result. According to the National Commission on Reading, "Classroom research suggests that the amount of time devoted to work sheets is unrelated to year-to-year gains in reading proficiency."[4] What is helpful, the Commission went on, is the amount of independent, silent reading children do in school. In fact, average minutes per day reading books is the best single predictor of growth in reading comprehension, vocabulary size, and reading achievement between the second and fifth grades.[5]

Other influences on students' academic performance may be too much time spent watching television, the breakup of the nuclear family, the changing socioeconomic mix of students, and school funding problems. As educators and concerned citizens, however, it behooves us to concentrate on those resources we do control and to make certain that they are employed to the fullest advantage.

Toward that end, literature has a key role to play in the school reform movement. The National Commission on Reading recommended that by the third or fourth grade, children should be reading independently a minimum of two hours per week. "Children's reading should include classics and modern works of fiction and nonfiction that represent the core of our cultural heritage," the Commission advised.[6] California's *Model Curriculum Standards, Grades Nine Through Twelve: English/Language Arts,* which was adopted and published in early 1985, emphasizes the importance of literature in much the same fashion. According to the introduction to the *Model*

---

[1]The sources for this quotation and others that appear within this chapter are on page 52.

Curriculum Standards, "Wherever we have looked, we have seen an answer to our education problems in returning students vigorously and intensively to the very core of English-Language Arts—to the literary works that reflect the meaning and values the human race decides are worth transmitting."[7] (See the appendix of the English-Language Arts section of the *Standards* for a list of recommended readings in literature.)

In addition to the *Model Curriculum Standards,* several other publications of the California State Department of Education are focused on strategies for teaching the English-language arts. (See *Handbook for Planning an Effective Writing Program; Practical Ideas for Teaching Writing as a Process; Recommended Readings in Literature, Grades Kindergarten Through Eight;* the *English-Language Arts Framework for California Public Schools, Kindergarten Through Grade Twelve;* and the *English-Language Arts Model Curriculum Guide, Kindergarten Through Grade Eight.*) The present handbook is the logical extension of these because it maintains that literature provides the best vehicle possible for teaching all the language arts: reading, listening, speaking, and writing. At the same time, literature is also tremendously valuable for its own sake. The great works in our literary canon reveal the noblest aspirations of the human spirit. They confront students with existential dilemmas that encourage the students' moral and ethical growth. They instruct even as they entertain.

The central purpose of this handbook is to promote the return to a literature-based English-language arts curriculum. The document is designed to provide useful information for all those responsible for improving the English-language arts course of studies, especially school-level planners, teachers, and parents. Towards that end, Chapter II describes the distinguishing characteristics of an effective literature program—the *what* of the handbook. Chapter II includes strategies for organizing the material for an effective program (by means of core, extended, and recreational reading programs), criteria for selecting individual works, and the key developmental issues at the various grade levels. Chapter III focuses on the teacher's role in a literature program—the *how* of the handbook. Chapter III also gives special attention to strategies for bringing a text to life and for presenting literature to limited-English-proficient students. Chapter IV addresses the indispensable support that is needed for an excellent literature program—in-service education for teachers as well as the involvement of parents in the program. Chapter V presents

". . . and we don't understand that life is heaven, for we have only to understand that and it will at once be fulfilled in all its beauty, . . ."

FYDOR DOSTOYEVSKY,
The Brothers Karamazov

a checklist that summarizes the main ideas of the handbook. Planners should find the checklist helpful in identifying the strengths and weaknesses of existing literature programs and in selecting strategies for change.

As a reader, you are urged to add your own insights to the suggestions found here. Only in that way will the literature program you devise truly reflect the range of local conditions and aspirations. For those interested in delving deeper into this topic, a list of references appears at the end of the handbook.

School reform is a cooperative effort or it is nothing at all. Restoring literature to the center of the English-language arts programs will require the common effort and hard work of tens of thousands of individuals at every level of the educational process— from curriculum planners to school district governing boards to teachers in the classroom. That effort is more likely to be forthcoming if all those involved are convinced of the importance of the task. Simply put, people work better towards a goal when it makes sense to them. For that reason, Chapter I begins with the most fundamental question of all: Why teach literature?

I

Why Teach Literature?

*Tavistock House,
Tavistock Square,
where Charles
Dickens lived from
1851 to 1860*

[The artist] speaks to our capacity for delight and wonder, to the sense of mystery surrounding our lives; to our sense of pity, and beauty, and pain; to the latent feeling of fellowship with all creation—and to the subtle but invincible conviction of solidarity that knits together the loneliness of innumerable hearts, to the solidarity in dreams, in joy, in sorrow, in aspirations, in illusions, in hope, in fear . . . which binds together all humanity—the dead to the living and the living to the unborn.[1]

JOSEPH CONRAD

Why should we teach literature to young people? What is so special about this body of material that we insist that all students be exposed to it? Joseph Conrad's eloquent statement suggests part of the answer: As no other discipline can, the study of literature invites us to peer deeply into the nature of our humanity, free from the habits imposed by fashion or personal experience, and to see ourselves and the world we inhabit in fresh perspective. In all candor, however, this classic liberalizing mission is not very compelling to those of a utilitarian bent. Why should students be required to waste their time reading poetry or fabricated stories, the skeptics ask, when there is so much practical knowledge available? Why? Because literature is eminently useful in its own right. As Clifton Fadiman observed, literature is one of those essential subjects that, once learned, help students to master all the rest. The study of literature is not just a matter of providing belles lettres for the college bound; the study of literature is basic for all students.

The Value of Teaching Literature

What exactly do we hope to accomplish by teaching literature? The answer is: several things at the same time. We expect that a well-conceived literature program will encourage the growth of students by increasing their appreciation of the aesthetic values of literature; by honing their intellectual skills; by developing their allegiance to the highest ideals of citizenship in a democracy; by refining their feelings, their personalities, and their relationships with others; and by deepening their sense of ethical responsibility. If all that sounds

[1]The sources for this quotation and others that appear within this chapter are on page 52.

ambitious, it should. Education proposes nothing less than leading students to the wisdom and virtue of the examined life and has never been an occupation for the faint of heart.

Promoting Aesthetic and Intellectual Growth

Considering the enumerated goals of a literature program one at a time, how can the study of literature contribute to each? First, literature promotes aesthetic and intellectual growth in several distinct ways. To begin at the most elementary level, literature is highly entertaining. Well-known childhood literary works, such as "Jack and the Beanstalk," the Anansi Spider tales, Maurice Sendak's *Where the Wild Things Are,* or Taro Yashima's *Crow Boy* are sure to capture children's imaginations. This proven ability to enchant is not to be dismissed lightly. Reading research shows that ". . . children usually read at a higher level . . . when they find a topic particularly interesting."[2] The desire to find out (or confirm) what happens next has an almost magical power to help pull a new reader through a story.

The paradox of teaching the skill of reading is that although the activity can be broken down into a number of discrete subtasks, in general the most useful form of practice is using the whole skill. But how can a child practice reading without already knowing how? A key part of the answer lies in motivation. Familiar stories that are easily understandable to the child, or even partly known by heart, are great enticements to the beginning reader.

Once students have entered the imaginative world conjured up by literary works, a series of intellectual benefits begins to accrue. Because of its emotional value, literature motivates reading, which leads to improved reading skills. Vocabulary expands. In grades three through twelve, for example, children learn the meaning of roughly 3,000 new words a year—most of these, researchers say, as the result of reading books or other materials.[3] Listening and speaking skills develop in class discussions. Writing improves. In each case, literature serves as a natural focus for helping students achieve greater language mastery. Furthermore, because literature can motivate reading, it can serve as a vehicle to encourage learning in other subject areas such as science, social studies, fine arts, and even physical education. For this reason all teachers in departmentalized schools should include appropriate literature in their courses.

As students read good books, they unconsciously assimilate the subtle variations of syntax, rhythm, and usage which stimulate and help refine their writing styles. It follows that schools should keep

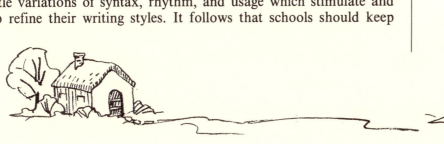

models of excellent writing in front of their students—novels, such as Charles Dickens's *Oliver Twist* or Rumer Godden's *The Mousewife,* which also happen to be masterpieces of prose style and penetrating insight into the human condition. In English classes, students are expected to read these provocative works, debate the momentous issues raised by them in class discussions, weigh the various interpretations, and come to their own conclusions in frequent written reports and papers. In all this, literature serves as an ideal matrix for teaching students how to think.

Developing a Sense of Citizenship

A second important benefit of the literature curriculum is that it fosters an awareness of society. The original argument for under-writing the expense of public education was that the survival of de-mocracy depended on it; either society would educate its new leaders or suffer the consequences. In school, citizenship is often perceived as the prime responsibility of the history teacher, but the teacher of literature has an important contribution to make in this regard as well. This is true because genuine citizenship entails more than instruction in the basic tenets of our social compact—the Bill of Rights, the separation of powers, the rule of law, and so on. It also involves making the emotional connections: developing in our children a sense of belonging, a loyalty to our past, and a willingness to participate in our future.

Building a Sense of Rootedness

Literature can help build the sense of rootedness. Take a central concept like the rule of law. A student might read *The Ox Bow Incident* by Walter van Tilburg Clark. In it, some angry ranchers catch a group of what they take to be cattle rustlers and, after finding some pretty damning circumstantial evidence, (and despite their pleas of innocence) hang them. But it turns out that the *rustlers* are innocent. The novel is an emotionally taut explication of why we do not tolerate vigilantism in our society. In the opposite direction, Arthur Koestler's *Darkness at Noon* portrays the nightmarish logic of a totalitarian state in which the objective guilt or innocence of the individual has become an irrelevancy. In either case, the student is invited to think about the institutions that distinguish a free society from an authoritarian one and the perils that accompany their abuse.

"True law, the code of justice, the essence of our sensations of right and wrong, is the conscience of society."

WALTER VAN TILBURG CLARK,
The Ox-Bow Incident

". . . that is happiness; to be dissolved into something complete and great. When it comes to one, it comes as naturally as sleep."

WILLA CATHER,
My Antonia

More than institutions, however, literature gives us human beings, and by dramatizing the past in human terms, shows us who we are as Americans and where we came from. A student who reads Willa Cather's *My Antonia* appreciates the sheer tenacity of the subsistence farm families who settled this country. The dour lineaments of Puritan New England live in Nathaniel Hawthorne's *The Scarlet Letter*, as do the bloody passions of the Civil War in Stephen Vincent Benet's *John Brown's Body* or Stephen Crane's *The Red Badge of Courage*.

The mental habits associated with the study of literature also help develop mature personalities. Education in a free society strives to create individuals capable of exercising good judgment and forming their own opinions as the ultimate expression of that freedom. The discipline good literature instills—of using language precisely—contributes to this goal. In a famous essay written just before his death, George Orwell argued that in modern, centralized society, a sensitivity to the use of language was no longer a requirement for professional writers alone; it was the very foundation of a healthy polity. The point is, a literate people are less likely to swallow propaganda or clever euphemisms masquerading as the truth and, as a result, make better citizens.

Developing Ethical Responsibility

The most far reaching impact from the study of literature, however, concerns the most searching of public education's goals: challenging each student to develop a personal sense of ethical responsibility. "Poetry essentially operates in the realm of values," Robert Lowell once wrote.[4] Poetry asks the big questions: What is the relationship of the individual to society? What criteria should guide a person's actions? What gives meaning to a man's or woman's life? In providing answers to these questions, authors do not sermonize but rather show psychologically plausible characters grappling with the force of circumstance and the consequences of their own acts. The novelist or playwright or poet does not tell the reader what is right or wrong; rather, the work of art puts readers in positions to perceive human nature in ways that they might otherwise have missed.

9

"On the breast of her gown, in red cloth, surrounded with an elaborate embroidery and fantastic flourishes of gold thread, appeared the letter A."

NATHANIEL HAWTHORNE,
The Scarlet Letter

In a fictional work, the reader is often invited to see the world through the eyes of the main characters. We take this imaginative step for granted, but it is a big leap. At the heart of most ethical systems—from the New Testament to Immanuel Kant's categorical imperative—is the notion of mutuality: Treat others as you would wish to be treated. But please note: By inducing the audience to identify with the experience of another, the dynamic of literature has already predisposed the reader to start thinking sympathetically. Literature encourages the reader to feel connected to the larger human community. It helps create that sense of empathy and shared human values that underpin all ethical action.

To be sure, literature should not take the place of the family, church, or other community institutions in forming character; its power is suggestive, not absolute. In his famous essay, "What Is Art?" Leo Tolstoy observed that the task of art is to make people good by choice. The qualifying phrase is significant. Literature can show the reader what good and evil look like. It can show the difference, in the words of the French essayist Michel de Montaigne, "between ambition and greed, loyalty and servitude, liberty and license."[5] But it cannot make us moral. A systematic exposure to our civilization's finest achievements in literature will ensure that students are confronted with the essential questions in life. How students answer them is, and must remain, up to them.

Arguments Opposing a Literature Program

Probably the most frequently cited reason for not putting literature at the core of the English curriculum is that such a program would be too tough for average and below average students. They would become bored or restless, and the dropout rate would increase sharply. Dedicated teachers and noteworthy schools have demonstrated that, in practice, just the opposite results. It is certainly true that the difficulty of reading selections must be matched to the aptitude of students; that the rate at which material is introduced may vary; and that some groups require special attention. But these are questions of means. The desired end—exposing students to a core of significant literary works—is too valuable to concede. (See the conclusion of Chapter III for suggestions on teaching literature to the less-prepared student.) Commitment to excellence is the key to success. As Vice-

10

Chancellor William Schaeffer advised teachers at the 1985 summer conference on literature held at the University of California, Los Angeles, "If you believe that what you are doing in your classroom is simply the most important thing going on in the universe at that moment, most of your students will believe it, too."

A second argument against the teaching of literature, which enjoyed greater currency in the late 1960s and 1970s than it does now, goes something like this: Literature is an "elitist" discipline, a subterfuge for imposing ruling-class values on oppressed groups so that they will cooperate in their own exploitation. According to this argument, minority students will encounter a world view in literature classes that is either irrelevant to their own heritage or downright destructive of it. The rebuttal to this argument is straightforward: It is wrong. The treasure-house of literature is not oppressive; it is liberating—of the constraints of time, place, and personal experience into which each of us as an individual is born. The real injustice would be to deny any child access to the wealth of insights that our best literature has to offer. To deny students the wisdom of our literary heritage may restrict their social mobility and limit the potential that schools have to create opportunities for students to develop their individual talents and to prepare for participation in our society.

Of course, in literature and the arts, local districts should adopt reading lists that recognize the natural desire of communities to maintain an ethnic identity. Quite rightly, black students are inspired by Alex Haley's *Roots* and Richard Wright's *Black Boy*; Hispanic students, by Rudolfo A. Anaya's *Bless Me, Ultima* and Peter Matthiessen's *Sal Si Puedes: Cesar Chavez and the New American Revolution*; Japanese-Americans, by Yoshiko Uchida's *Samurai of Gold Hill* and Monica Sone's *Nisei Daughter*; and so on. Like all great literature, these stories confer lasting benefits—intellectual, social, and spiritual—on those who read them. Furthermore, all students will profit from such literature to understand those whose experiences of America differ from theirs. The point is, far from being "elitist," the common culture belongs to all of us. And every child in the United States—rich or poor, male or female, black, Hispanic, Asian, or white—is entitled to experience it fully.

Our country was founded on the expectation that out of many traditions one nation could evolve that would be stronger and more durable than any single tradition. To argue that teaching a common

"Now, he could take his place next to Father and the other men, and would face any new disappointments without flinching."

YOSHIKO UCHIDA,
Samurai of Gold Hill

11

core of literature in our pluralistic society is not feasible because there is no basis for consensus is to beg the question. It is, and always has been, precisely the task of the public schools to help form that consensus.

In a society that celebrates the prerogatives of the individual, the public schools are potentially one of the most meaningful forces for social cohesion. They are the modern equivalent of the village square—a forum for identifying the shared ethos of our diverse and cosmopolitan society; a place where all our children can come together and discover what it is that unites us as a people. Well-taught literature is an essential part of that consensus building. How to achieve that great work—how to improve literature instruction in California's classrooms—is the subject of this handbook.

II

Profile of an Effective Literature Program

We have been so preoccupied with trying to find out how to teach everybody to read anything that we have forgotten the importance of what is read. Yet it is obvious that if we succeeded in teaching everybody to read, and everybody read nothing but pulp magazines, obscene literature, and Mein Kampf, *the last state of the nation would be worse than the first. Literacy is not enough.*[1]

ROBERT MAYNARD HUTCHINS

As Robert Hutchins suggests in the quotation above, not all specimens of the written word are equally potent in helping students reach the ambitious goals that were described in Chapter I for the study of literature. Therefore, certain questions need to be answered: Which books should be taught in school? What criteria are to be used in making the selections? What are the features of an effective literature program? In this chapter, some of the questions raised by Mr. Hutchins are considered, and some commonsense answers are proposed.

From a planning perspective, one effective way to structure the literature program is to divide it into three groups: core, extended, and recreational-motivational reading programs. The core list comprises a literary background that children in a given school or district hold in common. Briefly, the core program consists of central works in all literary genre which are given intensive attention on a classwide basis. Teachers help all students in a classroom experience these works through close reading and in other ways, such as hearing them read aloud in part or whole or seeing them performed on stage or screen. The point is that all students in a classroom, including those whose dominant language is not English, should experience the core literature program. Through the commonality of the core works, the students will be better prepared and motivated to participate in subsequent discussion, student writing, and other activities designed to help them more fully comprehend literature in general and the core works in particular. Curriculum planners, with the help of materials selection committees, can ensure that students experience a sequential and broadly representative sampling of our literary heritage by developing a list of core materials in all literary genre from which

[1]The sources for this quotation and others that appear within this chapter are on page 52.

teachers choose works to teach directly in the classroom setting. The number of works given such intensive attention cannot be great, given the constraints of time. Accordingly, the importance of the extended and recreational-motivational programs in literature should not be overlooked.

The extended program is composed of those works that the teacher recommends for students to read on their own time to supplement classwork. It is a particularly useful program for adapting to the special interests and abilities of individual students. By means of the extended program, for example, bright students can be challenged to delve deeper into the work of an author who has attracted their interest. Students who have difficulty reading can be directed to books that they find manageable and interesting. The extended program also offers a means for continuing student learning during the summer break.

The third type of literature program—the recreational-motivational reading program—focuses on the natural curiosity of students. In order for this type of program to work well, high-quality works of literature must be readily available in school and classroom libraries. These independent reading materials, which are recommended by teachers or librarians, need to be accessible to students during regularly scheduled library periods, as well as before and after school.

Most junior and senior high schools are departmentalized, with the teaching of literature almost entirely carried out by the English department. As mentioned earlier, students should have opportunities to experience literature as a vehicle for learning in other subject matter areas also, but teachers in English departments usually have the most responsibility for planning and organizing a school's literature program. There are a number of ways to structure such programs to ensure that students have literary experiences across the curriculum and that the core, extended, and recreational-motivational programs are related. Individual works can be grouped around a common theme—"family life," "war and peace," "the search for justice," and so on. They can be presented by genre (poetry, the novel, short stories, and so forth); by author (the plays of Shakespeare, essays of Henry David Thoreau, haiku of Matsu Basho); by historical period (American literature is often presented chronologically); by ethnic perspective (for example, the black experience, as distilled in the works of Richard Wright, Maya Angelou, James Baldwin, Lorraine Hansberry, James Langston Hughes, and Countee Cullen); or by region (the California of John Steinbeck, Robinson Jeffers, Francis Bret Harte, Richard Henry Dana, William Saroyan, John Muir, Sally Carrighar, and Kenneth Rexroth). At the elementary level readings in children's literature might be grouped in terms of categories such as picture books, folklore, modern fantasy, poetry, contemporary realistic fiction, historical fiction, and nonfiction.

The point is, no matter how the individual course is arranged, the effective literature program must be strategically coordinated from

"What happens to a dream deferred?
  Does it dry up
  like a raisin in the sun? . . .
Or does it explode?"

LANGSTON HUGHES,
Harlem

15

year to year—primary grades through high school—in order to achieve a cumulative result that is both broad and well-balanced. Specifically, this implies that planning the core list should take place not just within but also across grade levels. It follows that the years each student spends in the literature program from kindergarten through grade twelve should be conceived of as an articulated series of experiences.

The Core Program

Obviously, the core program forms the backbone of the literature program; and its development and success depend on one of the most significant planning decisions affecting the school curriculum, as expressed in this question: What should the list of titles for the core program include? Generally, the list should include those works that will foster in students the intellectual, social, aesthetic, and moral growth described in Chapter I.

As a starting point, the core list should be well-balanced in several respects. In terms of genre, it should include works from all of the major literary modes, including poetry, drama, fiction, and nonfiction. In terms of chronology, it should include enough old favorites to give a sense of the wealth of the written tradition as well as enough contemporary works to provide a sense of literature as an ongoing venture. In terms of breadth, it should represent the full range of human moods and voices (comic, romantic, tragic, satiric, melodramatic, and so on). Works by both men and women from around the world should be studied. Because the diversity of American society should be reflected in the literature program, it is imperative that excellent writing by authors from racial and ethnic minority groups be sought out and included. The common quality shared by selections should be their acknowledged literary worth—their power to raise questions, stimulate the imagination, provide a fresh point of view, and expand the student's knowledge of the world and of the possibilities inherent in language.

Criteria for Making Selections

The selections on the core list should represent the best that has been thought and said. However, reaching agreement on such a list is never easy, but in the give and take of a selection process sponsored by the school district, a consensus can be reached. In that effort, and putting aside issues of overall balance of the core list for the moment to focus on individual works, three fundamental criteria should be used to determine whether specific works should be placed on the list of books for the core program: suitability, content, and language use.

Suitability for Students. The first criterion to apply to potential book selections is to determine how suitable the books are to the students' general level of emotional and intellectual maturity. If, for instance, the works selected are generally beyond the readiness of students, it will take a particularly motivated and gifted teacher to help them understand and appreciate the works. On the other hand, each work should also present a realistic challenge to students, stretching their vocabulary and language skills and expanding their knowledge of the world.

Depth of Content. The second criterion concerns the matter of substance. Specifically, does the selection contain the compelling intellectual, social, or moral content to merit widespread study? E. D. Hirsch, Jr., of the University of Virginia has pioneered the notion of *cultural literacy*—the idea that there is a common fund of background knowledge in history, science, politics, language, and literature that every educated American is presumed to know. According to Mr. Hirsch, the technical skill of reading is like the tip of an iceberg; what actually makes possible the concise exchange of meaning from author to audience is a great mass of assumed prior knowledge that lies beneath the surface.

It follows from Mr. Hirsch's analysis that certain literary works should be read if for no other reason than that they are socially enabling. They acquaint students with a common vocabulary and ethical lore. They provide a culturally shared reference point from which questions of values, attitudes, and beliefs can be explored. As the National Commission on Reading has observed, "For each age [group], there are fables, fairy tales, [and] classic and modern works of fiction and nonfiction that embody the core of our cultural heritage. A person of that age cannot be considered literate until he or she has read, understood, and appreciated these works."[2] For a kindergartner, cultural literacy might mean knowing the story of *Goldilocks and the Three Bears* or *Peter Rabbit;* for an eighth grader, it might mean reading Owen Wister's *The Virginian* or Robert Louis Stevenson's *The Strange Case of Dr. Jekyll and Mr. Hyde;* for a high school senior, it might mean studying the poetry of John Keats or Arthur Miller's *Death of a Salesman.*

Defining the core list is the responsibility of the school district. Two pillars of Western culture deserve special consideration, however, whenever a list of literary works is being prepared. Students should encounter the plays of William Shakespeare at several points in their school career. Their experiences with these plays should not, however, be limited to silent reading on an individualized basis. They should also have opportunities to hear portions effectively read aloud and to view productions of them either live or as performed in films and videotapes. Also, they should have the opportunity to read the Bible as literature or at least those portions of it that are the most relevant to the study and understanding of literature. Among these texts might be Genesis, the Book of Job, the Psalms, the Epistles of St. Paul, and one of the Gospels. The Bible is the single most frequently quoted and alluded to book of the Western world, particularly in works of literature. For students to understand these references and allusions and their relevancy to a work being studied, they need some awareness of the Bible as it relates to and informs such literature.

Language Use. The third requirement for selecting a book for the core list is straightforward. It must be an example of excellent language use. However, that does not mean that only formal prose is acceptable. For example, e. e. cummings plays with language in ways that help students feel the fun of a world that is *mud-luscious* and *puddle wonderful.* Mark Twain shrived the soul of a nation with a hayseed vernacular in *The Adventures of Huckleberry Finn.* In each case, the language is fresh, inventive, apt, and, therefore, a worthy model for imitation. What students do not need put before them is poorly crafted literature whose purple prose, clumsy syntax, and hackneyed imagery provide them with the wrong models and may inhibit their growth in sensitivity to the effective use of language.

No matter how careful the deliberations, it is inevitable that occasionally a title on the core list will be challenged by one or more members of the community. To prepare for this eventuality, the school district should have a printed, board-adopted policy that spells out procedures to be followed when the use of a book is questioned. "The Students' Right to Read," a publication of the National Council of Teachers of English, and "The Library Bill of Rights" of the American Library Association outline workable policies. For instance, a literary selection that might raise community controversy if required as classroom reading may be acceptable without protest if offered as a reading option. (Both of these titles are listed under "Other Sources" in the "Selected References" section of this handbook.)

Another caveat for the selection committee is that in framing the core reading list, one should be sure to leave room for the teacher's discretionary judgment and creative inspiration. After all, in the final analysis, the classroom teacher is in the best position to gauge the intellectual and emotional maturity of a given group of students. Furthermore, the greater delight a teacher takes in a particular work, the better his or her chances are of arousing student interest in it. Enthusiasm in literature class, as in all subjects, is contagious. For these reasons, the core list should be structured so that at each grade level, the teacher is afforded a range of content choices. Once defined, the list should be regarded as a dynamic, not a static, concept. It should be reviewed regularly by all parties concerned to make sure new works and fresh perspectives are incorporated.

Mark Twain

Teaching Suggestions at Four Grade Span Levels

In the following section, the key issues in teaching literature at four educational levels are identified (kindergarten through grade three, grades four through six, grades seven through nine, and grades ten through twelve), and some titles and authors that work well at these age levels are noted. However, these ideas are not put forward as complete, detailed curricula; rather, they are meant to suggest something of the range and scope of an exemplary literature program. For kindergarten through grade eight, titles which are additional to those mentioned here can be found in the Department of Education's *Recommended Readings in Literature, Kindergarten Through Grade Eight*. This title is included in the "Selected References" in the Appendix of this handbook.

Teaching Literature in Kindergarten Through Grade Three. In the primary grades, children encounter literature mainly as it is told, read, or performed for them. This is an ideal time to engage in the time-honored tradition of storytelling. Teachers who tell stories will earn a special place in the hearts of their children; and this early exposure to oral literature will increase the children's attention span, listening vocabulary, the ability to visualize, and general cultural knowledge—all important prereading skills.

In the primary grades, literature also plays a key part in the early practice of reading itself. Reading research shows that the more closely a story fits an expected structure, the easier it is for children to understand.[3] Regrettably, most *stories* in primary basal textbooks (at least in terms of character, plot, motive, or resolution) do not tell a story at all. In fact, governed as they are by inflexible vocabulary and sentence-length restrictions, many basal texts barely seem to be written in standard English. Literature's great advantage over the basal texts is that children find the contents of the classic children's tales fascinating. Favorite stories can form a natural bridge to reading for the beginning student. Not only are such stories easier to digest because of their familiarity, but children also relish the added accomplishment of making them their own, of doing *real* reading for the first time.

In terms of specific recommendations, an effective program for the primary grades includes all the major literary forms. The infectious Mother Goose rhymes, strange happenings in Leslie Brooks's *Johnny Crow's Party,* or such cozy worlds as A. A. Milne's *When We Were Very Young* introduce children to the charm of versification. Whimsical inventions of Edward Lear or Kate Greenaway are presented alongside contemporary poetry by John Ciardi, Eve Merriam, or Shel Silverstein.

Traditional folktales offer a wealth of options for storytelling, reading aloud, or dramatic playacting. Of course, there is the celebrated collection of the Brothers Grimm (*Snow White and the Seven Dwarfs, The Brave Little Tailor, Little Red Riding Hood, Rumplestiltskin,*

"Where am I going? I don't quite know.
What does it matter where people go?
Down to the wood where the blue-bells grow—
Anywhere, anywhere. I don't know."

A. A. MILNE,
When We Were Very Young

A. A. Milne with Christopher Robin and Pooh in 1926

Hansel and Gretel, and so on); the modern fantasies of Hans Christian Andersen (*The Emperor's New Clothes, The Ugly Duckling, The Red Shoes);* or Aesop's Fables ("The Tortoise and the Hare," "The Fox and the Grapes"). Nursery tales with a cumulative development allow children to participate in the telling of stories (for example, *Chicken Little, The Three Billy Goats Gruff, Goldilocks and the Three Bears).* Modern equivalents with a similarly repetitive structure that children like include *Ask Mister Bear* by Marjorie Flack, *The Carrot Seed* by Ruth Krauss, and *In the Forest* by Marie Hall Ets. The Anansi Spider folktales from Africa, North American Indian legends, or tales from Japan, such as *The Funny Little Woman,* broaden the cultural base, as do Russian folktales set to music and dance. Superb renditions of *The Nutcracker* by Peter Illyich Tchaikovsky or *Peter and the Wolf* by Sergei Prokofiev are available on records and tape.

Animal stories, both fanciful and realistic, are also popular with children in the primary grades. Munro Leaf's delightful *The Story of Ferdinand*, Beatrix Potter's timeless *Peter Rabbit*, and Marguerite Henry's *Brighty of Grand Canyon* are outstanding examples. Roger Duvoisin, Don Freeman, Leo Lionni, Arnold Lobel, Bill Peet, and Marjorie Flack have written many such entertaining stories for students in the primary grades.

Fiction that comments on real-life situations is also an important ingredient of the early literature program. Bernard Waber's *Ira Sleeps Over* deals with the dilemma many kindergartners have faced: what to do with one's teddy bear on those occasions when one wants to act grown up. In *The Tenth Good Thing About Barney,* Judith Viorst poignantly describes a child's reaction to the loss of a family pet. Evaline Ness's *Sam, Bangs and Moonshine* and Eleanor Estes's *The Hundred Dresses* raise important social issues that upper-primary students can understand.

In terms of nonfiction, books that provide general information or illustrate concepts about the world have their place in a literature program for the primary grades. Tomie de Paola's *The Cloud Book,* Peter Spier's *People,* or Leonard Everett Fisher's *Star Signs* are good examples. Picture books, such as Donald Crew's *Freight Train* or *Harbor,* would complement an early social studies unit on transportation.

Undoubtedly, however, the most significant goal of the literature program in the early years is to show youngsters that books can be a source of intense enjoyment. Beginning in kindergarten, children should have the opportunity to explore books on their own. Good choices for this purpose include wordless picture books (Brinton Turkle's *Deep in the Forest,* Molly G. Bang's *The Grey Lady and the Strawberry Snatcher,* Mercer Mayer's *Boy, a Dog, and a Frog*); well-illustrated story books (*Alexander and the Terrible, Horrible, No Good, Very Bad Day* by Judith Viorst, *Circus* by Brian Wildsmith, *Anno's U.S.A.* by Mitsumasa Anno); and books designed to help children learn the alphabet and learn to count. Children at this grade level should be free to select books of their own and to go through them during silent, uninterrupted "reading" sessions. In the primary grades, the emphasis of this independent reading time is not on decoding the words on the page so much as giving children a sense of familiarity with books and the freedom to respond to them as they like.

Teaching Literature in Grades Four Through Six. By the time students have reached grade four, the majority of them have acquired the rudiments of reading and are eager to use this new tool to expand their understanding of the world. Encouraging this crucial transition (from learning to read to reading to learn) should be reflected in the core program for grades four through six. Specifically, it is particularly important in these years that schools offer imaginative and thought-provoking reading selections—in literature, science, history—to take advantage of children's natural curiosity at this age and to make certain this interest is sustained and rewarded. Unfortunately, research suggests that—far from seeking out original and stimulating materials—from 75 to 90 percent of what goes on during reading periods in elementary school classrooms simply follows the lead of the basal reading programs of national textbook publishers.[4] Students spend most of their "reading instruction" time filling out workbooks and skill sheets. For example, in one well-known study, out of 17,997 minutes of class time observed, "reading comprehension" instruction (beyond the perfunctory level of defining words) accounted for a total of only 45 minutes.[5]

An effective literature program in grades four through six can help break the cycle of endless workbook exercises and can help reduce significantly the number of bored and restless students who are not getting the type of instruction they need in the higher-order thinking skills. The program can achieve these things because literature, by its very nature, raises the issue of comprehension. When young children first read *Charlotte's Web* by E. B. White, for example, they encounter a yarn about a pig, a spider, and a rat. In point of fact, however, they will also be wrestling with some rather profound observations about the nature of friendship, loyalty, and unselfishness. To grasp this message, however, a child must interpret beyond the literal meaning, and that requires a certain facility in abstraction, language manipulation, and mental agility. Literature fosters this quantum leap in understanding. It invites both students and teacher to discuss the text, try to understand the intentions of the author, and express a point of view.

Compared to selections in the primary grades, the literature program in grades four through six is noticeably more sophisticated. It might include the use of acting scripts based on such works as Mark Twain's *Tom Sawyer*, Washington Irving's *Rip Van Winkle*, and even simplified portions of some of Shakespeare's plays. An example of the latter might be the comic scenes from *A Midsummer Night's Dream*. This introduction to drama as a form of literature can be enhanced by the use of reader's theatre as a classroom technique.

In place of nursery tales, students begin to relish characters with some psychological depth. In poetry, T. S. Eliot's *Old Possum's Book of Practical Cats* and Christopher Smart's *For I Will Consider My Cat Jeoffry* appeal to the tastes of children in the intermediate grades. Traditional ballads, such as "Barbara Allan" or "Sweet William's Ghost," evoke melancholy events of the past with an unadorned beauty. Reflections on childhood experiences—"Combing" by Gladys Cardiff and "If Mama" by Lucille Clifton—hold interest well. Even negative experiences provide food for thought (for example, Countee Cullen's "In Baltimore," a child's first contact with unreasoned prejudice; John Ciardi's "On Flunking a Nice Boy Out of School"; or Robert Hayden's "The Whipping").

Published poems by children of the same age also have a special appeal. The yearly anthology of the California Poets in the Schools or *The Poetry Connection*, a compilation of poems by Massachusetts students, are likely sources. Kenneth Koch's *Rose, Where Did You Get That Red: Teaching Great Poetry to Children* suggests many ways in which great poetry can be approached through imitation. Certainly, the discipline of writing poetry—hunting for the exact word, image,

T. S. Eliot

*"Glorious, stirring sight!" murmured Toad . . . "The poetry of motion! The **real** way to travel! The **only** way to travel! Here today—in next week tomorrow! Villages skipped, towns and cities jumped—always somebody else's horizons! O Bliss! O poop-poop! O my! O my!"*

KENNETH GRAHAME,
The Wind in the Willows

or metaphor to convey an impression—helps sensitize students to the nuances of language.

In terms of prose fiction, several types of stories appeal to children in the intermediate grades. Adventure stories in which a youngster plays a major part in the action are usually well received. (Robert Louis Stevenson's *Kidnapped*, Scott O'Dell's *Island of the Blue Dolphins*, Rudyard Kipling's *Kim*). Young readers enjoy such enduring flights of the imagination as Kenneth Grahame's *The Wind in the Willows*, L. Frank Baum's *The Wizard of Oz*, or Lewis Carroll's *Alice in Wonderland*. Adventure stories with a science fiction twist translate the fantasy tradition into modern settings (for example, Norton Juster's *The Phantom Tollbooth*, Madeleine L'Engle's *A Wrinkle in Time*, or Robert C. O'Brien's *Mrs. Frisby and the Rats of Nimh*).

A characteristically American form of folk literature that students enjoy at this age is the "tall tale"—usually the deliberately exaggerated exploits of a real (Johnny Appleseed, Mike Fink) or imagined (Paul Bunyan, Pecos Bill, John Henry, Old Stormalong) folk hero. Similarly, the myths and legends of ancient Greece are also eagerly absorbed; for example, Prometheus stealing fire from heaven; the labors of Hercules; Perseus and the Gorgon's head; and the wanderings of Odysseus. Across three millennia, children secretly sympathize with the hot-blooded willfulness of Phaethon driving the chariot of Apollo or the ecstasy of Icarus soaring upward on wings of wax. Sally Benson tells many of these wonderful stories in highly readable fashion in *Stories of the Gods and Heroes*. Ian Serraillier's more advanced version is well adapted to being read out loud.

Probably the most universally familiar form of literature for students in the intermediate grades is the animal story. There is, of course, the whole stable full of horse tales (led by Walter Farley's *The Black Stallion*), as well as such favorites as Felix Salten's *Bambi*, Joy Adamson's *Born Free*, or Marguerite Henry's *King of the Wind*. An increasing number of excellent books have been written that give a factual representation of the natural world; for example, see Jean

George's *Julie of the Wolves* for a vivid picture of the complex interactions of a wolf pack.

A trend in contemporary youth fiction is a willingness to portray the problems and concerns of children in modern society. *The Rare One* by Pamela Rogers describes a boy's difficult adjustment when a stepmother and stepsister join the household. *Queenie Peavy* by Robert Burch portrays small-town Georgia society and a thirteen-year-old's struggle for self-esteem. *Summer of the Swans,* a Newberry Medal winner by Betsy Byars, deals with mental retardation. Other worthwhile titles in this vein include *Dorp Dead* by Julia Cunningham, *Harriet the Spy* by Louise Fitzhugh, *North to Freedom* by Anne Holm, *A Girl Called Al* by Constance Greene, and *Freaky Friday,* a fantasy by Mary Rodgers.

High school students themselves might be enlisted to create reading motivational activities for the younger elementary students. To bring children's literature to life, the high school classes might present plays of tall tale heroes or one-person shows. To highlight the multicultural character of our country's folklore, the older students might tell stories to the primary classes, using folktales from our many peoples. Drawing their material from books, these students will motivate the younger children to read more on their own while acquiring a deeper appreciation of literature for themselves.

In the intermediate grades, an abundance of well-written novels can help children experience vicariously early American life. Esther Forbes's *Johnny Tremain* takes students through the main events of the Revolutionary War as a youth would have seen them. Laura Ingalls Wilder's *Little House* books describe family life on the frontier prairie. *Children of the Covered Wagon* by Mary Jane Carr tells of the trials pioneers endured crossing the American desert. Medieval England is also the scene for many fine children's books (for example, *The Door in the Wall* by Marguerite De Angeli or *Adam of the Road* by Elizabeth J. Gray).

Finally, biographies and autobiographies can provide children in the intermediate grades with models of individuals who have made significant cultural, religious, political, or scientific contributions. Isaac Bashevis Singer's *A Day of Pleasure: Stories of a Boy Growing up in Warsaw* is an excellent example. In it, the Nobel prize-winning author describes his becoming aware of life's realities as a youngster growing up in Warsaw. Other exemplary works of this kind could include Erik C. Haugaard's *Lief the Unlucky,* Barbara Brenner's *On the Frontier with Mr. Audubon,* Carl Sandburg's *Abe Lincoln Grows Up,* Lillie Patterson's *Frederick Douglass: Freedom Fighter,* and Jane Goodsell's *Eleanor Roosevelt.*

Teaching Literature at the Junior High School Level. In most junior high schools, the teaching of literature takes place in a departmental English program. In place of the self-contained classroom of the elementary years—with a single teacher handling instruction in all areas—students now have a different teacher for each subject. This specialization reflects the increasing complexity of the material students are now being asked to absorb. It also implies a new seriousness of purpose. During this period of adolescence, students waver on the threshold of the adult world—childlike in their outlook one moment, impatient for more responsibility and independence the next. They are going through an impressionable time of life and can greatly benefit from the wisdom and experience available in our best literature.

With regard to content, at these grade levels students should not receive the impression that poetry is pretty but insincere. They should encounter verse that explodes cliches (Shakespeare's "Sonnet 130," "My Mistress' Eyes Are Nothing Like the Sun," or Gwendolyn Brooks's "We Real Cool"); that tickles the funny bone (see Ogden Nash's *Parents Keep Out: Elderly Poems for Youngerly Readers*); and that takes seriously the transition from childhood to young adulthood (for example, Ezra Pound's "The River Merchant's Wife: a Letter" or William Stafford's "Fifteen"). As William Wordsworth wrote, the wellspring of poetry is "emotion recollected in tranquility"; and poems that interpret actual experience help heighten the students' own growing powers of sensory observation (for example, Wordsworth's "Sonnet: Composed Upon Westminster Bridge, 3 September 1802," or Pablo Neruda's "Ode to a Fallen Chestnut."[6]

The short story is a particularly accessible teaching medium in grades seven through nine. Many outstanding authors whose novels would be too difficult for most students at this stage are perfectly manageable in smaller helpings. Consider, for example, D. H. Lawrence's "The Rocking Horse Winner," F. Scott Fitzgerald's "The Diamond as Big as the Ritz," or James Joyce's *Dubliners*. From Washington Irving, Edgar Allan Poe, and O'Henry to the contemporary works of John Cheever or Shirley Jackson, no form has shown literary genius to better advantage than the short story.

Novels that students of this age enjoy tend to be action-oriented (Jack London's *The Call of the Wild,* C. S. Forester's *Captain Horatio Hornblower* series, Alexandre Dumas's *The Count of Monte Cristo*) or genre types (classic westerners like Owen Wister's *The Virginian* or Jack Schaefer's *Shane,* the well-crafted mystery stories of Sir Arthur Conan Doyle, or romances such as Charlotte Bronte's *Jane Eyre*). However, works of serious social commentary are also well received (for example, Jessamyn West's *Massacre at Fall Creek,* the story of the first white man tried for killing an Indian in the United

Jessamyn West

"Literature is my Utopia. Here I am not disfranchised. No barrier of the senses shuts me out from the sweet, gracious discourse of my book friends. They talk to me without embarrassment or awkwardness."

HELEN KELLER,
The Story of My Life

States; Harper Lee's *To Kill a Mockingbird;* Monica Sone's *Nisei Daughter).* Nonfiction writing that shows examples of real life and moral purposefulness is especially worthwhile at a period when students are just beginning to search out their own values (for example, Thor Heyerdahl's *Kon-Tiki,* Helen Keller's *The Story of My Life,* Maya Angelou's *I Know Why the Caged Bird Sings,* John F. Kennedy's *Profiles in Courage).*

Junior high school students are also ready for another taste of the theater. Perhaps the opportunity will present itself for reading and then viewing Thornton Wilder's *Our Town,* William Gibson's *The Miracle Worker,* or William Shakespeare's *Romeo and Juliet.* To give a feeling for the recurring nature of certain literary ideas, the teacher might present a whole portfolio of ill-fated romantic entanglements— from Heloise and Abelard to the Yosemite legend of the naming of Half Dome and Lost Arrow. The unit might conclude with students viewing the film version of the *West Side Story* and discussing points of comparison with Shakespeare's *Romeo and Juliet.*

In any event it is most important that junior high school students become "hooked on books," since this period may be their last chance to become motivated, self-directed readers. Many students who have not become genuinely interested in reading by the time that they leave the eighth grade have little likelihood of ever doing much reading.

Teaching Literature at the Senior High School Level. The high school years are, as Joel J. Kupperman has observed, *"par excellence* a time of orienting oneself in the central goals and purposes of one's life."[7] In its organization, content, and teaching strategies, an effective high school literature program should help promote this quest for values. By the time students have entered high school, they have enough command of language and life experience to benefit from the subtle and morally demanding themes of mature literature. Challenging novels, drama, poetry, and nonfiction can now be read and contemplated in all their insight, passion, and evocative power (for example: such novels as James Agee's *A Death in the Family,* Ralph Ellison's *Invisible Man,* Joseph Conrad's *Heart of Darkness,* and Franz Kafka's *The Metamorphosis;* dramatic works like *Oedipus Rex, Hamlet,* and *The Glass Menagerie;* the poetry of John Milton,

Alexander Pope, W. B. Yeats, and T. S. Eliot; and such nonfiction as Henry David Thoreau's *Civil Disobedience,* Martin Luther King's "I Have a Dream," and Lewis Thomas's *The Lives of a Cell: Notes of a Biology Watcher*). The *Model Curriculum Standards: Grades Nine Through Twelve—English/Language Arts,* adopted by the California State Board of Education on January 11, 1985, include several hundred suggested titles for a core and extended literature program. Beyond this list, only one or two observations need to be made.

The first observation concerns the danger of relying too heavily on anthologies, collections of short fiction and verse that serve as literature textbooks in many classrooms. An anthology has its virtues because it can put a great deal of material serving curricular goals in front of students at a reasonable cost. On the other hand, when used by themselves, anthologies also send students the wrong message. They imply that literature is defined in terms of whatever fits between the covers of one canonized volume. But a literature class should be a voyage of discovery, not a commuter trip. Paperback editions of outstanding works of prose and poetry should also be introduced whenever possible to heighten the student's sense of the richness and variety of the literary world awaiting their investigation.

The second advisory in organizing the high school literature program concerns the desirability of cross-disciplinary planning. Particularly in the nonfiction category, many beautifully written works central to the various academic disciplines—history, mathematics, biology, and so on—are equally worth studying in a literature class as examples of clear expository prose. One thinks of Alexis de Tocqueville's *Democracy in America,* J. B. S. Haldane's "On Being the Right Size," or Charles Darwin's *The Descent of Man.* Cross-disciplinary coordination makes sense. After all, the student who reads Galileo Galilei's *The Starry Messenger* is going to learn from one source something about astronomy, the intellectual currents impelling the Catholic reformation, and the rules of rational discourse. Knowledge is not easily partitioned. A little organizational effort can ensure

"I have a dream that my four little children will one day live in a nation where they will not be judged by the color of their skin, but by the content of their character."

MARTIN LUTHER KING,
Speech at Civil Rights March on Washington [August 28, 1963]

that these felicitous intellectual activities can happen with regularity; as an example, students could study the unexpurgated Jonathan Swift's *Gulliver's Travels* in English class at the same time that they are learning about England's social revolution in a history class.

A Summary of the Core Program

In summary, the selection of a core reading list is a crucial step in the development of an effective literature program. In compiling the core list, some planning criteria are constant—those of appropriateness, balance, and excellent language use. Other criteria vary with the age group.

Broadly speaking, in the primary grades, the key issue is making sure that literature is an integral and enjoyable part of the daily classroom routine. In grades four through six, the key issue is using the appeal of literature to promote the transition from reading as a mechanical skill to reading for knowledge and emotional reward. At the junior high school level, the departmental literature program usually begins, and a key issue is making certain that the program is strategically planned to provide a good basic foundation and that it meshes smoothly with the high school program. At the senior high school level, the literature program should help initiate students into the adult world by acquainting them with "the best that has been thought and said" in the history of our civilization.

Extended Literature Program

The second part of an effective literature program is the extended reading program, which incorporates those works that the teacher encourages students to read on their own time to supplement classwork. Obviously, no matter how well organized the core program is, time permits only relatively few works to be read closely and discussed by the class as a whole. The extended program copes with this limitation by doing just what it says: It extends awareness of our vast literary heritage by inviting students to read great books independently.

Several techniques are employed in the extended reading program. Two or three times a week the teacher gives a short "book talk," a five-minute sketch of a recommended book. The talk might feature a few intriguing details about the author, a dramatic reading of an excerpt from the text, or storytelling based on the text. Students who accept the invitation are rewarded in the early years by having their names posted on "bookworm forms" that are posted in the classroom; in later school years they may be given extra credit as a reward.

Another extended reading technique involves the use of oral reports. Several students who have read the same book can present a panel discussion about it in front of the whole class. To make certain they use the class time well, the students should meet on their own beforehand, choose a discussion leader, and write down the questions they intend to answer about the book. As a variation of this technique, students at the secondary level may use the panel discussion approach, but this time each student on the panel has read a different book, but with some common thread (author, period, narrative point of view, and so forth). The panel members discuss points of similarity and divergence and read passages aloud to illustrate their arguments. After the presentation, members of the class are invited to ask questions about the books.

Another worthwhile element in the extended literature program is the summer reading plan. The long summer months can have a regressive effect on academic skills. One way to prevent this academic backsliding over these months is to conduct a well-run summer reading program. The ingredients are simple: a list of recommended titles (paperbacks available in local public libraries, book stores, or on long-term loan from the school library); a modest share of the student's vacation time; and parental cooperation. Obviously, this last element is crucial and should be courted assiduously throughout the school year. In "open house" remarks, PTA conferences, school and local newspaper articles, telephone "trees," and direct mail, the reasons for the summer program should be clearly explained and the active participation of parents recruited.

Here is one way to organize such a program. In June, students are issued a list of suggested readings, together with student/parent response forms corresponding to the number of books to be read. (Five books over the summer months would be a reasonable minimum.) After reading each book, the student completes the form, summarizing the book's contents and his or her reaction. A parent reviews this paragraph and then asks a few questions about the book (initiating an enjoyable conversation). Once satisfied that the child has read the book, the parent dates and signs the response form in the space provided. In September, teachers collect these forms and credit students in a way that the teaching staff has agreed is appropriate.

The success of the summer reading program is largely a matter of building the expectation—among teachers, parents, and students—that the reading will be done. Once established, the summer reading program pays large scholastic dividends.

Recreational-Motivational Program

The third part of an effective literature program is the recreational-motivational phase. Establishing this phase of the program is more

"But I do not want people to call me a fool, and if my head stays stuffed with straw instead of with brains, as yours is, how am I ever to know anything?"

L. FRANK BAUM,
The Wizard of Oz

a matter of creating a school atmosphere that encourages a curiosity about books than it is a *program* per se. The recreational-motivational program can take many forms, but its indispensible starting point is the ready availability of high-quality reading materials in school and classroom libraries.

Research has confirmed the importance of easy access to books in fostering a positive attitude toward reading.[8] According to the National Commission on Reading, "in one study with non-native English speakers, ample classroom libraries were associated with dramatic improvements in reading achievement that were still evident when the children were retested a few years later."[9] Another study found that the summertime reading gains of children from poor households were related to the distance they lived from a public library.[10] In an effective literature program, a well-stocked school library, open before and after school as well as during the day, is not a frill; it is a necessity. Classroom libraries for which materials are carefully selected provide additional resources for students.

In an effective literature program, the library budget is safeguarded as a matter of districtwide board policy. The resourceful school staff may also wish to seek donations from the PTA, organize book swaps and book fairs, and develop an understanding with the local used-book store as creative ways of acquiring additional materials for school or classroom library collections. If careful selection criteria are maintained, the results are well worth the effort. School and classroom libraries not only give students a glimpse of the richness and variety of the literary world, but they also demonstrate in the most direct way possible that they have a claim on and an entree into that world, too.

Taken together, high-powered core, extended, and recreational-motivational reading programs guarantee that students receive a thorough grounding in our culture's literary heritage, which is what Robert Maynard Hutchins was calling for at the outset of this chapter. In the next section, the complementary issue of classroom technique— the role of the teacher in bringing the subject matter to life—is considered.

III

The Teacher's Role
in the Program

Accepting a summary of a poem, an analysis of someone else's reading or interpretation or experience of it, is analogous to having someone else eat your dinner for you . . . a work of art, as art, must be a personal experience.[1]

LOUISE M. ROSENBLATT

Teaching literature is fundamentally different from teaching the other academic subjects. It is different because, before it is anything else, literature is an art form. As such, a text in literature makes a direct claim on the emotions and imaginations of students. In social studies or chemistry classes, a body of information can be accurately conveyed in a didactic manner—by lecture or demonstration. In a literature class, however, the most valuable lessons cannot be imparted by proxy. A poem, short story, or novel comes to life only when readers turn their full attention to it. The implication of all this is that in a literature class, the focus should be on the relation between the student and the text. The teacher's role is to deepen, enrich, and clarify the quality of the students' responses, as advocated by Louise Rosenblatt and other proponents of the "response theory" for the teaching of literature.

The Teacher's Responsibilities

Carrying out the task of making the response to literature more meaningful is a balancing act. On the one hand, teachers should not insist on their students' embracing a single *correct* interpretation of a text. Coming into class the day after a reading assignment with a *here's-what-it-meant* lecture denies students a chance to explore a work for themselves. The intent should be to show students how to read a literary work with sensitivity and confidence—preparing them for a lifetime of enjoyment with books—not to make them dependent on a classroom authority figure for their opinions. On the other hand, it is also true that all student responses in a literature class are not equally germane, reasonable, or even honest. Teachers who indiscriminately praise every comment, no matter how farfetched or unfounded, eventually diminish the value of their approval.

Insofar as the background knowledge that the teacher has—facts about the author, period, literary tradition, form, or structure—

---

[1]The sources for this quotation and others that appear within this chapter are on page 52.

contributes to better understanding, it should be freely drawn on. Learning such information, however, is not a worthwhile end in itself. One does not need to know the difference between an alexandrine and a catalexis, for example, to appreciate good poetry. But when studying a sonnet, it helps a high school student to know that the term *sonnet* refers to a recurring form of fourteen lines of iambic pentameter. In general, the technical vocabulary of literary analysis (terms like *hyperbole, onomatopoeia,* or *denouement*) is best introduced, as the need arises, in the context of a piece of literature that exemplifies it.

The best literature teachers are those who create an atmosphere of trust in class discussions, who listen attentively to each student's comments, and then draw out consequences by means of probing questions. Gifted teachers start with the response to a text as they find it in their classrooms—excitement, disgust, pity, ambivalence—and build on that to lead students to a deeper engagement with the claims of the author. A guiding principle might be that any number of interpretations of the meaning of a work are valid as long as the reader can support his or her idea on the basis of language in the text. While different points of view are expected, respect for the opinion of the individual is the bedrock value. In the normal course of reading a work, disagreements lead back to the text—to a closer look at what the author has to say on the subject. Such teaching is facilitated by and grounded on an integrated program in which all elements of English-language arts are taught in concert with literature as their core.

In measuring student achievement in the literature program, teachers must be very careful in selecting their methods of assessment. By its very nature literature is not particularly amenable to objective testing. Such testing tends to peg the level of inquiry at a relatively shallow level. Objective testing may be useful in providing quick checks regarding student progress, but such tests should not constitute the main means for assessing student achievement in the literature program. Far more useful and revealing are subjective modes of assessing student achievement. If the higher goals of a response-based literature program and the attendant development by students of higher-level thinking skills are to be realized, then subjective evaluation of student progress should predominate. Shallow testing programs in the areas of literature will tend to encourage shallow thinking and a shallow understanding of the works students encounter. Far more revealing are subjective evaluations, such as essay tests, oral and written reports, anecdotal records kept by teachers, student responses to questions, and the quality of classroom discussion.

The Students' Rights and Responsibilities

In a sense, the response theory is a literary bill of rights. It affirms that all students have the inalienable right to their own thoughts, feelings, likes, and dislikes in coming to grips with a work of art. Rights, however, also confer responsibilities. Having affirmed that the teacher cannot experience a piece of literature for students, it becomes incumbent on students to do so for themselves. And this implies a good-faith effort.

Reading literature is not the passive absorption of a steady stream of ready-made images; it entails the engagement of the mind. In an era often jaded by shallow video entertainment, many students are not accustomed to making this extra effort. But conscientious teachers insist that they do. After all, labeling a work "boring" is not a response so much as it is a symptom of intellectual torpor. The fact is that any piece of writing will be boring—inert, lifeless—as long as the reader withholds his or her active mental engagement. However, students cannot be expected to like every literary selection presented to them. Nevertheless, they should be required to articulate in some depth just why they dislike a selection. Their ability to do so with flair and precision could well be one measure of their achievement in the literature program.

Of course, the whole idea of the core list is to select literary works that will attract students' interest and reward study. Beyond choosing the core reading list carefully, teachers can promote a student's engagement with literature by making explicit the connection between literature and the student's own life.

Activities for the Three Stages of Study

In designing lessons around major literary works, teachers should include activities suitable for use at three stages of study—before, during, and after the reading. Prereading activities should ignite student curiosity about the upcoming selection and fill in the necessary background (about the author, time period, or any specialized vocabulary). Before starting *Roll of Thunder, Hear My Cry,* for example, the teacher might read excerpts from the Newberry Award acceptance speech by Mildred Taylor as she shares the experiences that prompted her to write her highly acclaimed book. Before reading *Crow Boy* by Taro Yashima, students might talk about the experience of coming to a new school. Storytelling is an excellent way for quickening the interest of students in literature, with fine opportunities to enhance their listening skills as well. After such experiences, students can be motivated to read further the works of writers they have encountered in this dramatic fashion.

Activities during reading should be calculated to promote comprehension, cause students to compare responses, and call attention to graceful and effective uses of language. At the elementary level, that means asking basic questions at appropriate intervals in the reading, such as: What sort of person is the main character? How can you tell? What is the biggest problem he or she faces? If you were in his or her shoes, what would you do? These basic questions that promote comprehension sound simple enough, but it is just this sort of inquiry that builds proficiency in reading and yet occurs all too infrequently in elementary school classrooms.

In the later school years, the questions about literature become more searching, and the language skills they evoke become more sophisticated. In *Hamlet,* for instance, the soliloquies serve as a focal point for understanding the melancholy Dane's character. Students can dramatically render the soliloquies in oral readings, giving them a distinct interpretation: madness, naiveté, consuming revenge. The class then discusses which version seems to fit best. In terms of cultivating language awareness, while reading a short story such as "Home Run" by Lorenz Graham, students might list the regional colloquialisms used in the conversation between the farm boy and city folk, and then try substituting standard English. Which version is more colorful and alive?

After a reading assignment, classroom activities should be geared to focus and deepen the students' responses to the text and open up vistas that encourage long-term interest in literature. As already mentioned, making the connection between a text and real life—in class discussions, writing assignments, panel formats—is a particularly effective way to achieve this result. Original writing may also provide a good outlet for expression. Students enjoy writing imitations or parodies of favorite works (for example, W. H. Auden's "Unknown Citizen" might be reborn as the "Unknown Eleventh Grader"). In the schoolwide context, any forum to recognize student writing acts as leaven for the entire program (for example, a literary magazine or book reviews published in the school newspaper). Indeed, all students should be given opportunities to engage in writing in various genres and in a variety of modes of discourse. What better way is there to come to a full realization of what constitutes excellence in literary writing? By trying such writing, students begin to understand more fully the artistry of successful authors and poets.

Students should also be made aware of literature as an ongoing adventure to which they have access. For instance, well over 100 readings, poetry films, or dramatic/performance poetry productions are offered in the San Francisco Bay Area each month.

Literature for Limited-English-Proficient Students

Students who are classified as limited-English proficient (LEP) may not possess the English language skills necessary to digest the literary selections used in the regular classroom. Some of these read at levels far below grade-level expectations. Others are not fluent in English. A number of strategies can be pursued to bring these students into contact with literature and the vital lessons available from the great works. First, teachers should take responsibility for finding and employing appropriate materials. For LEP students, that generally means building the core program around less complex and sometimes shorter works—those that can be read and responded to in one or two class periods. Poetry, in particular, with its inventive use of language and concentrated format, lends itself to close reading in small doses. Longer works can be introduced by reading sections aloud in class or role-playing the conflict, encouraging students to continue on their own. The use of films, tapes, recordings, and other media as adjuncts to the literature program is also useful in motivating LEP students to participate.

For students of English as a second language, the teacher can substitute a translation of a classic. While they continue to upgrade their knowledge of English, students reading *A Tale of Two Cities* in Spanish, for example, will be fulfilling many of the goals of the literature program. Another possibility is to have these students read Gabriel García Márquez's *Chronicle of a Death Foretold* (*Crónica de una muerte anunciada*) or Carlos Fuentes's *A Change of Skin* (*Cambio de piel*) in the original while the rest of the class reads these works in translation. Teachers should also avail themselves, when possible, of bilingual aides, tutors, and resource teachers to help students needing language assistance to read selections in English.

For both the limited-English-speaking and English-as-a-second-language students, the reading program should be augmented with appropriate and well-designed listening and speaking activities. These activities could be assigned before, during, and after the reading of the literary work. To accomplish these activities, teachers and bilingual educators should develop storytelling, oral recitation, and dramatic presentations.

A Program's Most Important Ingredient

In the end, however, the most important ingredient in a successful literature program cannot be programmed or planned; it is the love of the word—contagious enthusiasm to share its power and magic as it is wrought into its highest art form—literature. That is the mark of the outstanding literature teacher. These individuals know the incredible value of the subject matter they teach and are convinced that every child can learn from works of literature. In the next chapter, we consider how an effective literature program supports dedicated teachers, with a plan to involve parents in the reading progress of their children and with a well-funded in-service training program.

IV

Aids to an Effective
Literature Program

*Jack London's study,
which was reproduced
in the House of
Happy Walls, built in
1916, near Glen Ellen,
California*

You may have tangible worth untold,
Caskets of jewels and coffers of gold,
Richer than I you can never be,
I had a mother who read to me.[1]

STRICKLAND GILLILAN

J ust as, ideally, the love of literature extends beyond the years of formal schooling, so too an effective literature program is complemented by forces outside the classroom. This chapter concerns three of the most important of these aids: parental support, in-service teacher education, and the school library/ media center.

Parental Support for the Literature Program

The research is unequivocal: A child's homelife makes a significant contribution to later interest in reading. As the Report of the National Commission on Reading summarized the evidence, "Most children will learn *how* to read. Whether they *will* read depends in part upon encouragement from their parents."[2] The process begins in infancy as parents tell stories and read aloud to their children before youngsters are able to read for themselves. Successful young readers tend to come from families in which many books and magazines are made available and frequent opportunities are given to visit libraries. Parents who want to help their children develop a taste for literature can do so by following these suggestions:

- Continue to read aloud to them even after they have learned to read. (Lewis Carroll's *Jabberwocky* is a delight to hear at any age.)
- Set an example for your children by reading regularly yourself.
- Have as many books and periodicals as possible in your home.
- Keep a good, up-to-date dictionary on hand and use it.
- Play vocabulary building games, such as Scrabble, Boggles, or crossword puzzles with your children.
- Instead of using simplified vocabulary in conversation, pause to explain difficult words.
- Take your children to the public library frequently.
- Turn off the commercial television, or turn to a public broadcasting station.

[1]The sources for this quotation and others that appear within this chapter are on page 53.

This last point above requires qualification. When television is viewed in moderation (up to ten hours a week), the evidence seems to suggest that it can be a genuine addition to the intellectual development of a child.[3] However, left to their own devices, most children will not be moderate in their viewing habits. More likely, children quickly approach the obsessive. The average sixth grader may spend more hours in front of a television set than in a classroom.

Parents should be aware of the negative effect that excessive television viewing may have on students' academic performance. The *California Assessment Program Annual Report 1985-86* showed the effects of time spent reading for pleasure, doing homework, and watching television on reading test scores of students in grades six, eight, and twelve. Results indicated that higher reading test scores occurred among students who spent "more time reading for pleasure and doing homework and less time watching television. . . ."[4] These results are not surprising, granted what we have already observed about the nature of cognitive development. All real learning is active, but commercial television mesmerizes much of its audience into becoming passive image consumers. Parents are responsible for intervening on behalf of a more demanding, and rewarding, form of entertainment— books—and for ensuring that their child's television viewing stays within reasonable limits.

Will most parents guide their child's television viewing? According to a 1984 Gallup Poll, when asked what the biggest problem facing the public schools was, teachers ranked "lack of parental involvement" at the top.[5] Why talk about parental support in this manual, then, when what parents do or fail to do is not under the school's control? The short answer is that if help from the home can benefit a child's education, it automatically becomes the public school's concern. Furthermore, experience shows that when they try, school districts can successfully elicit parental involvement. For example, in 1984 the Oakland Unified School District in Oakland, California, increased attendance at parent-teacher conference nights from 15 to 65 percent of all parents by means of a carefully orchestrated campaign. Backed by a network of telephone volunteers, editorials in the local newspaper, and guest appearances by school officials in the pulpits of 120 local churches on Parent Education Sunday, the district gathered several thousand pledges from parents promising to do the following things: spend a half hour of quiet time a day with their

Herman Melville

children, with television, stereo, and telephone all unplugged; make sure their children had a quiet place to do their homework; set a bedtime of no later than 9 p.m. for elementary schoolchildren; and take part in parent-teacher conferences.[6] These steps pertain to the whole educational process, not just literature, but they do suggest a willingness to support the schools. In terms of focusing on literature, the summer reading program outlined in Chapter II is an excellent place to start parental involvement and to educate parents concerning the impetus they can give to their child's reading progress.

In-Service Teacher Education

In-service education for teachers is another indispensable complement to an effective literature program, provided the training is focused on the day-to-day concerns of the literature instructor and is not devoted merely to school administrative matters. The chief desideratum for in-service education is that it should focus on the subject matter the teacher is teaching. Literature teachers need help in several ways:

- Rekindling their enthusiasm for the subject they teach
- Enlivening the core syllabus with new selections or imaginative juxtapositions of old ones
- Sharing successful classroom strategies with peers
- Feeling themselves part of an ongoing community of inquiry and scholarship

Unfortunately, the modern schoolteacher feels isolated, trapped in the classroom, and cut off from intellectual stimulation. In Japan teachers work a longer school year—220 days—but a full third of this time is spent working with peers on how to improve the quality of their instruction and the curriculum. In California more of this use of time is needed. However, new staff development efforts in the state are promising. The early results of programs such as the California Literature Project, the California Writing Project, and the state's Mentor Teacher Program have been encouraging. They suggest that some of the most effective in-service education takes place when teachers are allowed to provide for their own needs by participating in the planning of the effort and by experiencing peer teaching and demonstrations provided by experienced teachers. The cost—a seminar room, a reading list of paperback books, refreshments, a visiting professor serving as a facilitator and discussion leader, and released time for the participants—are manageable, and the dividends to faculty morale and classroom performance are substantial.

The School Library/Media Center

Another essential component of a successful literature program, the school library/media center, provides an environment that can motivate students and nurture and extend the literature program. What resources should the library/media center provide?

If we agree that the textbook is not the sole answer to instructional needs, then it is vital that the library collection provide a wide variety of literature, carefully selected to reflect student interests and abilities and the curricular emphasis of the instructional program. Resources available in the collection can also provide exciting ways for presenting literature in visual and aural, as well as in printed, forms. In addition to its variety, it is important that the library/media collection be vital and changing and that thoughtful selections be made from the thousands of materials published and produced each year. Because of the relatively high cost of many audiovisual materials, library/ media specialists can also assist in making informed decisions regarding their procurement for shared collections housed in such locations as school district offices and offices of county superintendents of schools. Needless to say, library/media specialists and classroom teachers may need to be trained to engage in such activities, including the establishment of materials selection criteria.

How can the staff of the school library/media center support and help implement the curriculum? As the teacher plans instruction for the literature program, the library/media center staff can provide resources for motivating, developing, and extending learning in such ways as providing the following:

- Audiotapes and recordings of readings from the works of authors being studied such as Robert Frost, John Steinbeck, William Shakespeare, Rudyard Kipling, Stephen Vincent Benet, Hans Christian Anderson, Charlotte Chorpenning, and Tomie De Paola
- Videotapes and films of performances of literary works such as the British Broadcasting Corporation's (BBC's) Shakespeare series, Ambrose Bierce's *The Occurrence at Owl Creek Bridge,* Shirley Jackson's *The Lottery,* and Marjorie K. Rawlings's *The Yearling*
- Information for teachers and students about impending performances of literary works on television and in local movie houses and live theatres
- The complete work from which a textbook excerpt has been taken
- Other works by or about the author
- Works on a related topic or theme
- Information that makes characters more understandable and makes settings come alive

Bateman's, Burwash, East Sussex, where Rudyard Kipling lived from 1902 to 1936

In the library, students who have been motivated by initial contacts with a literary work can be guided to other sources that will extend their interest. The library also provides the resources and ideas that invite the use of literature as a bridge to other areas of the curriculum: studying history through a novel; reading essays about unresolved issues in science; and matching poetry to music and painting.

How should the school library/media center be used? It should be accessible to students and teachers. This requires that the library be open and inviting, that its use be actively encouraged, and that institutional barriers for its use be minimized. A warm, welcoming environment can help to foster the climate for a community of readers. Students who are encouraged to enjoy and investigate literature independently in such an environment become lifelong readers.

How should the library/media center be staffed? Since there are no state requirements for the staffing of school libraries, there can be many levels of service, support, and leadership, depending on the priorities and budget limitations of each school district. Staffing might run the gamut from volunteers to part-time aides to trained technicians to professional library/media specialists or a combination of all of these. As a basic requirement, any staffing plan should provide a warm environment with a stress on literature. Ideally, a professional school librarian should be a literature expert who can provide considerable leadership in motivating students and implementing literature programs at a very sophisticated level. Such a person could facilitate the provision of help to students with special needs, the organization of book clubs, the procurement and distribution of literary materials, and the staff development of teachers of literature.

In concluding this brief discussion of the school library/media center, it seems appropriate to consider its involvement with the other two elements mentioned in this section: parental support and teacher in-service education. Parents can provide school media centers with substantial volunteer support; in return, these centers can provide parents with assistance, encouragement, and resources for their children. Teachers can look to the media center as well, not only for assistance in designing instruction but also for in-service education on what it contains. Book reviews, book lists, media previews, and demonstration lessons by library/media center staff are among the in-service training aids that the library/media center can provide.

Whatever is done to improve or enhance the services of the school library/media center must be done as a cooperative venture among parents, teaching staff, library personnel, and administrators. Funding sources should be thoroughly explored and priorities examined to foster the achievement of acceptable goals in this area. Several legitimate funding sources are now available in addition to the regular school budget: special grants, both federal and state; portions of the annual state textbook entitlement; local educational foundations; and support groups. With energy and vision, some of these sources can be tapped, and a significant impact can be made on the schoolwide literature program.

V

Checklist for Assessing a School's Literature Program

Although the following checklist is based largely on the preceding text, those who use it may wish to augment it with items based on other readings, such as those in the "Selected References," and also unique local needs. The checklist is not, and cannot be, exhaustive. Rather, it is intended as an illustration of an assessment tool that may need to be further refined and developed locally.

Readers should think of any such checklist as a means for reviewing a school's literature program in order that they might become more aware of the program's strengths and possible weaknesses. It can also be useful in helping them plan, develop, and implement a new program, as appropriate. In any event, however, it should never be used as a teacher evaluation instrument.

Indeed, if such checklists are improperly used, they can be intimidating and ultimately counterproductive. To avoid this, those who use this checklist should first read the preceding text and, possibly, other pertinent publications. Then they should consider what they learn in the light of what may be unique local problems and needs. Finally, prior to embarking on the assessment of the literature program in a school, they might first establish a spirit of collegiality regarding the effort. If a sense of ownership of solutions to possible areas of need can be established, the use of assessment instruments, such as this or a similar checklist, will be far less threatening to those it was designed to help.

I. Profile of an Effective Literature Program

	Ineffective	Somewhat effective	Effective	Very effective

A. The Core Program (See pages 16—28 of the text.)

How effective is your literature program in providing for:

1. A locally determined "core" list of works to be taught at each grade span level?   ___ ___ ___ ___

2. The inclusion in the core list at each grade span level of selections from each major literary area, including poetry, fiction, nonfiction, and drama, as appropriate to the age levels of students?   ___ ___ ___ ___

3. A well-balanced list of core works in terms of genre, chronology, breadth (comedy, tragedy, satire), works authored by both men and women, and works authored not only by well-known traditional literary figures in the English-speaking world but also by authors from other cultures and from racial and ethnic minority groups in our society?   ___ ___ ___ ___

4. The use of three fundamental criteria in selecting works for the core list, including suitability for age groups, substance leading to "cultural literacy," and examples of excellence in language use as opposed to trite, poorly crafted selections?   ___ ___ ___ ___

5. A printed, board-adopted policy that spells out procedures to be followed should the selection of a particular work on the core list be questioned by a member of the public? ___ ___ ___ ___

6. A core list that is broad enough to leave room for the discretionary judgment and creative inspiration of individual teachers (e.g., several novels at a grade level from which teachers can choose)?   ___ ___ ___ ___

7. A sense of ownership of the core list by involving in its development all professional staff who will be affected?   ___ ___ ___ ___

8. A systematic, well-organized core program in which the overlap of selections at more than one grade span level is avoided?   ___ ___ ___ ___

9. The development in departmentalized schools or grade levels of cross-disciplinary planning, which ensures that some of the works in the core program are worthy of study and applicable in more than one curricular area?   ___ ___ ___ ___

10. Programs in which basal readers and literature anthologies do not constitute the entire literature program, but are extensively augmented by the use of trade books and paperbacks?   ___ ___ ___ ___

	Ineffective	Somewhat effective	Effective	Very effective

11. Allocation of adequate classroom time to the core program, as opposed to programs in which the overuse of such mechanistic devices as workbooks and work sheets monopolize the time?

12. A core program in which all students have some experience with the Bible as literature and also with the works of William Shakespeare; if not in print, at least in viewing performances or hearing parts of the works read aloud?

13. The development and maintenance of adequate communication with students' parents to ensure that there is a general understanding of the core literature program and how it relates with the extended and the recreational-motivational readings in literature programs?

B. The Extended Literature Program
(See pages 28—29 of the text.)

How effective is your literature program in providing for:

1. A locally determined "extended" list of works available for students to select from and read on their own under the guidance of classroom teachers?

2. A well-balanced list of works for the extended program in terms of genre, chronology, breadth (comedy, tragedy, satire), works authored by both men and women, and works authored not only by well-known traditional literary figures in the English-speaking world but also by authors from other cultures and from racial and ethnic minority groups in our society?

3. A printed, board-adopted policy that spells out procedures to be followed should the selection of a particular work on the extended list be questioned by a member of the public?

4. An extended list of works available to students that is broad enough to provide them choices in the selections they wish to pursue while at the same time maintaining the teacher-determined extended nature of the program?

5. A sense of ownership of the extended list by involving in its development all professional staff who will be affected by it?

	Ineffective	Somewhat effective	Effective	Very effective

6. The development in departmentalized grade levels or schools of cross-disciplinary planning, which ensures that some of the works in the extended program are worthy of study and applicable in more than one curricular area? ____ ____ ____ ____

7. The development and maintenance of adequate communication with student's parents to ensure that there is a general understanding of the extended literature program and its relationship with the core and the recreational-motivational readings in literature programs? ____ ____ ____ ____

8. Employment of techniques, such as teachers' reading aloud from or giving brief oral sketches about selections from the extended list, students' oral reports or panel presentations about works that they have read, the establishment of summer reading programs, and the awarding of credit, as appropriate, as a way for motivating students to read works from the extended list? ____ ____ ____ ____

C. The Recreational-Motivational Program
(See pages 29—30 of the text.)

How effective is your literature program in providing for:

1. An atmosphere in the school in general, but in the school library in particular, which encourages a curiosity about books and the habit of reading? ____ ____ ____ ____

2. Classroom libraries to augment, but not replace, the school library? ____ ____ ____ ____

3. The establishment of ties with the school library and its staff and with local public libraries and librarians in support of the school's recreational-motivational reading program? ____ ____ ____ ____

4. The development of a program by means of which older students foster the interest of younger students in reading through presentations, such as plays, puppet shows, readings, and storytelling? ____ ____ ____ ____

5. A program of rewards by means of which students can earn credit for extra reading that they do on their own? ____ ____ ____ ____

6. A program of teachers' modeling reading for pleasure through such activities as daily periods of uninterrupted sustained silent reading? ____ ____ ____ ____

7. The scheduling from time to time of book swaps and book fairs as a means of fostering book ownership? ____ ____ ____ ____

II. The Teacher's Role in the Program

(See pages 32—36 of the text.)

	Ineffective	Somewhat effective	Effective	Very effective

How effective is your literature program in providing for:

1. The creation of a classroom atmosphere in which students do not feel intimidated about expressing their honest responses to works of literature? _____ _____ _____ _____

2. The recognition by classroom teachers of literature that their chief role is to deepen and enrich the quality of students' responses to literature? _____ _____ _____ _____

3. The encouragement of students' personal responses to literature, which they can justify, and the avoidance of imposed, single, "correct" interpretations? _____ _____ _____ _____

4. Classroom discussion and student writing in various modes of discourse that help students discover relationships between literature and their own lives? _____ _____ _____ _____

5. Lessons dealing with major literary works that feature activities suitable for use at three stages of study which occur before, during, and after reading? _____ _____ _____ _____

6. An integrated program in which all elements of English-language arts are taught in concert with literature as their core? _____ _____ _____ _____

7. The development of a literature program suitable to the needs of students whose dominant language is not English? _____ _____ _____ _____

8. Frequent opportunities for students to hear literature, in general, and poetry and drama, in particular, read aloud and orally interpreted by teachers, students, and recorded artists? _____ _____ _____ _____

9. The skillful use of probing questions by teachers as a means for helping students arrive at a better understanding of literary works? _____ _____ _____ _____

10. A program for assessing student achievement in literature in which objective testing is deemphasized and subjective assessment, such as essay tests, anecdotal records, oral and written reports, and the evaluation of the quality of student discussion, is emphasized? _____ _____ _____ _____

11. A schoolwide program by means of which students receive recognition for their excellent literary writing? _____ _____ _____ _____

12. The recognition by all teachers of literature that the basic underlying goal of the literature program should be to foster among students an ongoing lifelong interest in literature and the habit of pursuing it on their own? _____ _____ _____ _____

III. Aids to an Effective Literature Program

(See pages 38—42 of the text.)

	Ineffective	Somewhat effective	Effective	Very effective

A. Parental Support for the Literature Program

How effective is your literature program in:

1. Soliciting the help of parents of students in your school?

2. Soliciting parents to attend a school's open house and parent-teacher conferences?

3. Urging parents to read aloud to their children?

4. Urging parents to have many reading materials in the home and to do more reading themselves in the presence of their children?

5. Urging parents to take their children to local public libraries and to help them obtain library cards?

6. Encouraging parents to support a school's summer reading program for students?

7. Asking parents to monitor the quantity and quality of television programs viewed by their children?

8. Urging parents to establish an atmosphere in the home that is conducive to the study of literature?

B. In-service Teacher Education

How effective is your literature program in providing for:

1. The involvement of classroom teachers in planning and implementing in-service education programs?

2. The use of existing statewide in-service education programs, such as the California Literature Project, the California Writing Project, and the state's Mentor Teacher Program?

3. Teacher-to-teacher staff development programs in efforts to upgrade instruction and curriculum?

4. Classroom visitations by trusted and knowledgeable peers to ensure that teachers are applying what they have learned in staff development programs?

5. A system of released time for staff development purposes?

6. Policies to ensure that staff development programs are focused on the substance of teaching and curriculum in literature and not on extraneous matters?

	Ineffective	Somewhat effective	Effective	Very effective

7. An atmosphere of professional endeavor under which teachers do not feel isolated but cooperatively seek to improve a school's literature program?

C. The School Library/Media Center

How effective is your literature program in providing for:

1. A school library/media center that is open to students both before and after school and during the school day?

2. A trained school library/media specialist who does not merely perform clerical tasks but works directly with students to motivate them to read?

3. A library budget that is adequate for continued accessions and for the maintenance of a collection of at least ten volumes per student in the school and a commensurate number of films, videotapes, and recordings of literary works?

4. An atmosphere and environment in a school library/media center that is warm, welcoming, and yet businesslike?

5. A school library/media program in which accessibility is paramount and institutional and administrative barriers are minimized?

6. Accession policies which ensure the establishment of a broad variety of books, periodicals, and media items selected after thoughtful consideration?

7. A professional library on campus for teachers of literature?

8. Policies to ensure that library staffing is commensurate with the size of the school?

9. Policies to ensure that the responsibilities of the school library/media specialist include the in-service education of teachers of literature, occasional demonstration teaching featuring techniques such as storytelling, and planning with teachers to ensure that the school library/media program extends the classroom literature program?

Appendix

Notes

Foreword

1. Allen Tate, "The Present Function of Criticism," in *Essays in Modern Literary Criticism.* Edited by Ray B. West, Jr., New York: Holt, Rinehart and Winston, 1961, p. 146.

Introduction and Overview

1. David P. Gardner and others. *A Nation at Risk: The Imperative for Educational Reform. An Open Letter to the American People.* Washington, D.C.: National Commission on Excellence in Education, U.S. Department of Education, 1983, p. 18.
2. *Becoming a Nation of Readers: The Report of the Commission on Reading.* Prepared by Richard C. Anderson and others. Washington, D.C.: The National Institute of Education, U.S. Department of Education, 1985, p. 74.
3. Ibid., p. 74.
4. Ibid., pp. 75-76.
5. Ibid., p. 77.
6. Ibid., p. 119.
7. *Model Curriculum Standards, Grades Nine Through Twelve, English–Language Arts.* (First edition). Sacramento: California State Department of Education, 1985, p. E-1.

I Why Teach Literature?

1. *Joseph Conrad on Fiction.* Edited by Walter F. Wright. Lincoln: University of Nebraska Press, 1964, p. 161. Used with permission from the publisher.
2. *Becoming a Nation of Readers: The Report of the Commission on Reading.* Prepared by Richard C. Anderson and others. Washington, D.C.: The National Institute of Education, 1985, p. 91.
3. Ibid., p. 77.
4. Patrick Welsh, "The Role of Values in Teaching Literature in the High School," in *Challenges to the Humanities.* Edited by Chester E. Finn, Jr., Diane Ravitch, and P. Holley Roberts. New York: Holmes and Meier Publishers, Inc., 1985, p. 150.
5. *The Autobiography of Michel de Montaigne.* Edited by Marvin Lowenthal. Boston: Houghton Mifflin Co., 1935, p. 33.

II Profile of An Effective Literature Program

1. Robert Maynard Hutchins, *Education for Freedom.* Baton Rouge: Louisiana State University Press, 1943, pp. 14-15. Used with permission from the publisher.
2. *Becoming a Nation of Readers: The Report of the Commission on Reading.* Prepared by Richard C. Anderson and others. Washington, D.C.: The National Institute of Education, U.S. Department of Education, 1985, p. 61.
3. Ibid., p. 66.
4. Ibid., p. 35.
5. Ibid., p. 73.
6. William Wordsworth, "Preface to the Second Edition of the *Lyrical Ballads,*" in *English Romantic Poetry and Prose.* Edited by Russell Noyes. New York: Oxford University Press, 1956, p. 365.
7. Joel J. Kupperman, "The Teaching of Values," in *Challenges to the Humanities.* Edited by Chester E. Finn, Jr., Diane Ravitch, and P. Holley Roberts. New York: Holmes and Meier Publishers, Inc., 1985, p. 129.
8. *Becoming a Nation of Readers: The Report of the Commission on Reading.* Prepared by Richard C. Anderson and others. Washington, D.C.: The National Institute of Education, U.S. Department of Education, 1985, p. 78.
9. Ibid., pp. 78-79.
10. Ibid., p. 78.

III The Teacher's Role in the Program

1. Louise M. Rosenblatt, "A Way of Happening," *Educational Record,* Vol. 49, n. 3 (Summer, 1968), 340-341. Used with permission from the publisher.

IV Aids to An Effective Literature Program

1. Strickland Gillilan, "The Reading Mother," in *The Best Loved Poems of the American People*. Edited by Hazel Felleman. New York: Doubleday & Company, Inc., 1936, p. 376. Used with permission from the publisher.
2. *Becoming a Nation of Readers: The Report of the Commission on Reading*. Prepared by Richard C. Anderson and others. Washington, D.C.: The National Institute of Education, U.S. Department of Education, 1985, p. 26.
3. Ibid., p. 27.
4. *California Assessment Program Annual Report 1985-86*. Sacramento: California State Department of Education, 1986, p. 36.
5. Alec Gallup, "The Gallup Poll of Teachers' Attitudes Toward the Public Schools," *Phi Delta Kappan,* Vol. 66, n. 2 (October, 1984), p. 99.
6. "Quality Education Parent Pledge for Improving Student Achievement" (Oakland Unified School District, Oakland, Calif., 1984, Mimeographed).

Selected References

A great deal has been published regarding the teaching of literature. However, only those books that are cited in the text and that are particularly pertinent to the content of this handbook appear here. Many noteworthy publications on the subject are not listed, but only because they did not seem appropriate for the handbook's purposes. The references are divided into the following five groups: "Book Lists," "Books on Teaching Literature," "Literature Cited in the Text," "Literary Criticism and Theory," "Literary Research," and "Other Sources."

Book Lists

Adventuring with Books: A Booklist for Pre-K—Grade 6. Edited by Mary L. White. Chicago: American Library Association, 1981.

Adventuring with Books, 1985: A Booklist for Pre-K—Grade 6. Edited by Dianne L. Monson. Urbana, Ill.: National Council of Teachers of English, 1985.

Baskin, Barbara H, and Karen H. Harris. *Books for the Gifted Child.* New York: R. R. Bowker, Co., 1981.

Books for You: A Booklist for Senior High Students. Edited by Robert C. Small, Jr. Committee on the Senior High School Booklist. Urbana, Ill.: National Council of Teachers of English, 1982.

Braken, Jeanne, and others. *Books for Today's Young Readers: An Annotated Bibliography of Recommended Fiction for Ages 10–14.* Old Westbury, N.Y.: The Feminist Press, 1981.

Carlsen, G. Robert. *Books and the Teenage Reader: A Guide for Teachers, Librarians, and Parents* (Second edition). New York: Harper & Row Pubs., Inc., 1980.

Carr, Jo. *Beyond Fact: Nonfiction for Children and Young People.* Chicago: American Library Assocation, 1982.

Celebrating Children's Books: Essays on Children's Literature. Edited by Betsy Hearne and Marilyn Kaye. New York: Lothrop, Lee and Shepard Books, 1981.

Dreyer, Sharon S. *Bookfinder: A Guide to Children's Literature About the Needs and Problems of Youth Aged 2 to 15.* In two volumes. Circle Pines, Minn.: American Guidance Service, Inc., 1981.

Glazer, Joan I. *Literature for Early Childhood.* Columbus, Ohio: Charles E. Merrill Publishing Co., 1981.

Glazer, Joan, and Gurney Williams III. *Introduction to Children's Literature.* New York: McGraw-Hill Book Co., 1979.

Guide to Non-Sexist Children's Books. Compiled by Judith Adell and others. Chicago: Academy Chicago Publishers, 1976.

Guide to World Literature. Edited by Warren Carrier and Kenneth Oliver. Urbana, Ill.: National Council of Teachers of English, 1980.

Huck, Charlotte S. *Children's Literature in the Elementary School* (Third edition). New York: Holt, Rinehart & Winston, Inc., 1979.

Kimmel, Margaret M., and Elizabeth Segel. *For Reading Out Loud! A Guide to Sharing Books with Children.* New York: Dell Publishing Company, Inc., 1984.

Literature and Young Children. Edited by Bernice E. Cullinan and Carolyn W. Carmichael. Urbana, Ill.: National Council of Teachers of English, 1977.

McLean, Andrew M. *Shakespeare: Annotated Bibliographies and Media Guide for Teachers.* Urbana, Ill.: National Council of Teachers of English, 1980.

Rabkin, Norman. *Shakespeare and the Common Understanding.* New York: Free Press, 1967.

Recommended Readings in Literature, Kindergarten Through Grade Eight. Sacramento: California State Department of Education, 1986.

Schon, Isabel. *Hispanic Heritage: A Guide to Juvenile Books About Hispanic People and Cultures.* Metuchen, N.J.: Scarecrow Press, Inc., 1980.

Sebesta, Sam L., and William Iverson. *Literature for Thursday's Child.* Palo Alto, Calif.: Science Research Associates, 1975.

Sharing Literature with Children: A Thematic Anthology. Edited by Francelia Butler. New York: Longman, Inc., 1977.

Stanford, Barbara D., and Karima Amin. *Black Literature for High School Students.* Urbana, Ill.: National Council of Teachers of English, 1978.

Stensland, Anna L. *Literature by and About the American Indian: An Annotated Bibliography.* Urbana, Ill.: National Council of Teachers of English, 1979.

Sutherland, Zena, and others. *Children and Books* (Sixth edition). Glenview, Ill.: Scott, Foresman & Co., 1981.

Your Reading: A Booklist for Junior High and Middle School Students. NCTE, Committee on the Junior High and Middle School Booklist and Jane Christensen. Urbana, Ill.: National Council of Teachers of English, 1983.

Books on Teaching Literature

Becoming a Nation of Readers: The Report of the Commission on Reading. Prepared by the Commission on Reading. Washington, D.C.: U.S. Department of Education, 1984.

Committee on Literature in the Elementary Language Arts and Linda Lamme. *Learning to Love Literature: Preschool Through Grade Three.* Urbana, Ill.: National Council of Teachers of English, 1981.

Cook, Elizabeth. *Ordinary and the Fabulous* (Second edition). New York: Cambridge University Press, 1976.

Dunning, Stephen. *Teaching Literature to Adolescents: Poetry.* Glenview, Ill.: Scott, Foresman & Co., 1966.

Dunning, Stephen. *Teaching Literature to Adolescents: Short Stories.* Glenview, Ill.: Scott, Foresman & Co., 1968.

Farrell, Catharine H. *Word Weaving: A Guide to Storytelling.* San Francisco, Calif.: Zellerbach Family Fund, 1983.

How Porcupines Make Love. Edited by Alan C. Purves. New York: John Wiley & Sons, Inc., 1972.

Koch, Kenneth. *Rose, Where Did You Get That Red: Teaching Great Poetry to Children.* New York: Random House, Inc., 1974.

Koch, Kenneth, and Kate Farrell. *Sleeping on the Wing: An Anthology of Modern Poetry with Essays on Reading and Writing.* New York: Random House, Inc., 1982.

Lamme, Linda L., and others. *Raising Readers: A Guide to Sharing Literature with Young Children.* New York: Walker & Co., 1980.

Literature for All Students: A Sourcebook for Teachers. Prepared by the California Literature Institute Participants. Los Angeles: The Office of Academic Interinstitutional Programs, University of California, Los Angeles, 1985. (Available from the publisher.)

Lukens, Rebecca J. *Critical Handbook of Children's Literature* (Second edition). Glenview, Ill.: Scott, Foresman & Co., 1982.

Miller, Bruce E. *Teaching the Art of Literature.* Urbana, Ill.: National Council of Teachers of English, 1980.

Model Curriculum Standards, Grades Nine Through Twelve. Sacramento: California State Department of Education, 1985.

Model Curriculum Standards, Grades Nine Through Twelve—English/ Language Arts. Sacramento: California State Department of Education, 1985.

Norton, Donna E. *Through the Eyes of a Child: Introduction to Children's Literature.* Columbus, Ohio: Charles E. Merrill Publishing Co., 1983.

Probst, Robert E. *Response and Analysis: Teaching Literature in the Secondary Schools.* Upper Montclair, N.J.: Boynton/Cook Publishers, Inc., 1987.

Purves, Alan C., and Dianne L. Monson. *Experiencing Children's Literature.* Glenview, Ill.: Scott, Foresman & Co., 1984.

Rockas, Leo. *Ways In: Analyzing and Responding to Literature.* Montclair, N.J.: Boynton Cook Publishers, Inc., 1984.

Sloan, Glenna D. *Child As Critic: Teaching Literature in the Elementary and Middle Schools* (Second edition). New York: Teachers College Press, Columbia University, 1984.

Sloyer, Shirlee. *Reader's Theatre: Story Dramatization in the Classroom.* Urbana, Ill.: National Council of Teachers of English, 1982.

Stewig, John W. *Informal Drama in the Elementary Language Arts Program.* New York: Teachers College Press, Columbia University, 1983.

Stewig, John W. *Read to Write: Using Children's Literature as a Springboard for Teaching Writing* (Revised edition). New York: Holt, Rinehart & Winston, Inc., 1980.

Teaching Literature in Grades Seven Through Nine. Edited by Edward B. Jenkinson and Jane S. Hawley. Ann Arbor, Mich.: Books on Demand, 1967.

Teaching the Epic. Edited by Margaret Fleming. Urbana, Ill.: National Council of Teachers of English, 1974.

Trelease, Jim. *Read-Aloud Handbook.* New York: Penguin Books, Inc., 1985.

Weber, J. Sherwood. *Good Reading: A Guide for Serious Readers.* New York: New American Library, 1980.

Literary Criticism and Theory

Bleich, David. *Readings and Feelings: An Introduction to Subjective Criticism.* Urbana, Ill.: National Council of Teachers of English, 1975.

Booth, Wayne C. *Critical Understanding: The Powers and Limits of Pluralism.* Chicago: University of Chicago Press, 1979.

Brower, Reuben A. *Fields of Light: An Experiment in Critical Reading.* Westport, Conn.: Greenwood Press, 1980.

Gardner, John C. *On Moral Fiction.* New York: Basic Books, Inc., 1978.

Holland, Norman N. *Five Readers Reading.* New Haven, Conn.: Yale University Press, 1975.

Only Connect: Readings on Children's Literature. Edited by Sheila Egoff and others. New York: Oxford University Press, Inc., 1980.

Reader-Response Criticism: From Formalism to Post-Structuralism. Edited by Jane P. Tompkins. Baltimore, Md.: Johns Hopkins University Press, 1981.

Rosenblatt, Louise M. *Literature as Exploration* (Third edition). New York: Modern Language Association of America, 1983.

Rosenblatt, Louise M. *Reader, the Text, the Poem: The Transactional Theory of the Literary Work.* Urbana, Ill.: National Council of Teachers of English, 1978.

Slatoff, Walter J. *With Respect to Readers: Dimensions of Literary Response.* Ithaca, N.Y.: Cornell University Press, 1970.

Wellek, Rene, and Austin Warren. *Theory of Literature.* New York: Harcourt Brace Jovanovich, Inc., 1956.

Wellek, Rene. *A History of Modern Criticism: 1750 to 1950.* In four volumes. New York: Cambridge University Press, 1983.

Literary Research

Applebee, Arthur N. *Child's Concept of Story: Ages Two to Seventeen.* Chicago: University of Chicago Press, 1978.

Purves, Alan C., and Richard Beach. *Literature and the Reader: Research in Response to Literature, Reading Interests and the Teaching of Literature.* Urbana, Ill.: National Council of Teachers of English, 1972.

Squire, James R. *Responses of Adolescents While Reading Four Short Stories.* Urbana, Ill.: National Council of Teachers of English, 1964.

Steiner, George. *After Babel: Aspects of Language and Translation.* New York: Oxford University Press, Inc., 1975.

Literature Cited in the Text

Adamson, Joy. *Born Free.* New York: Random House, Inc., 1974.

Aesop's Fables. In four volumes. Edited by Kathryn T. Hegeman. New York: Trillium Press, 1984.

Agee, James. *A Death in the Family.* New York: Bantam Books, Inc., 1971.

Anansi the Spider: A Tale from the Ashanti. Retold and Illustrated by Gerald McDermott. New York: Holt, Rinehart & Winston, Inc., 1972.

Anaya, Rudolfo A. *Bless Me, Ultima.* Berkeley, Calif.: Tonatiuh/Quinto Sol International, Inc., 1976.

Andersen, Hans Christian. *The Emperor's New Clothes.* Mahwah, N.J.: Troll Assocs., 1979.

Andersen, Hans Christian. *The Little Match Girl.* Boston: Houghton Mifflin Co., 1968.

Andersen, Hans Christian. *The Red Shoes.* Morton Grove, Ill.: Coach House. Press., Inc., 1969.

Andersen, Hans Christian. *The Ugly Duckling.* Mahwah, N.J.; Troll Assocs., 1979.

Angelou, Maya. *I Know Why the Caged Bird Sings.* New York: Bantam Books, Inc., 1971.

Anno, Mitsumasa. *Anno's U.S.A.* New York: Putnam Publishing Group, 1983.

Auden, W. H. "Unknown Citizen" in *Sounds and Silences: Poetry for Now.* Edited by Richard Peck. New York: Dell Publishing Co., Inc., 1970.

Bang, Molly. *The Grey Lady and the Strawberry Snatcher.* New York: Scholastic, Inc., 1980.

"Barbara Allan" in *Words in Flight: An Introduction to Poetry.* Edited by Richard Abcarian. Belmont, Calif.: Wadsworth Publishing Co., 1972.

Baum, L. Frank. *The Wizard of Oz.* New York: Putnam Publishing Group, 1956.

Benet, Stephen V. *John Brown's Body.* Cutchogue, N.Y.: Buccaneer Books, 1982.

Benson, Sally. *Stories of the Gods and Heroes.* New York: Dial Books for Young Readers, 1940.

Brenner, Barbara. *On the Frontier with Mr. Audubon.* New York: Putnam Publishing Group, 1977.

Bronte, Charlotte. *Jane Eyre.* New York: Bantam Books, Inc., 1981.

Brooke, Leslie L. *Johnny Crow's Party.* New York: Frederick Warne and Co., Inc., 1907.

Brooks, Gwendolyn. "We Real Cool" in *Contemporary American Poetry.* Edited by A. Poulin, Jr. Boston: Houghton Mifflin Co., 1970.

Brothers Grimm. *The Brave Little Tailor.* Mahwah, N.J.: Troll Assocs., 1979.

Brothers Grimm. *Cinderella.* New York: Greenwillow Books, 1981.

Brothers Grimm. *Hansel and Gretel.* New York: Dial Books for Young Readers, 1980.

Brothers Grimm. *Little Red Riding Hood.* Mahwah, N.J.: Troll Assocs., 1981.

Brothers Grimm. *Rumpelstiltskin.* Mahwah, N.J.: Troll Assocs., 1979.

Brothers Grimm. *Snow White and the Seven Dwarfs.* New York: French & European Pubns., Inc., n.d.

Burch, Robert. *Queenie Peavy.* New York: Viking-Penguin, Inc., 1966.

Byars, Betsy C. *Summer of the Swans.* New York: Penguin Books, Inc., 1981.

California Poets in the Schools. Edited by Katharine Harer, Gail Newman and Sarah Kennedy. San Francisco: California Poets in the Schools, 1982.

Cardiff, Gladys. "Combing" in *Carriers of the Dream Wheel: Contemporary Native American Poetry.* Edited by Duane Niatum. New York: Harper & Row Pubs., Inc., 1975.

Carr, Mary J. *Children of the Covered Wagon* (Revised edition). New York: Thomas Y. Crowell Junior Books, 1957.

Carroll, Lewis. *Alice in Wonderland.* Cutchogue, N.Y.: Buccaneer Books, 1981.

Cather, Willa. *My Antonia.* Boston: Houghton Mifflin Co., n.d.

Chicken Little. New York: Putnam Publishing Group, 1986.

Chorpenning, Charlotte B. *The Adventures of Tom Sawyer.* (Children's Theatre Playscript Series). Morton Grove, Ill.: Coach House Press, Inc., 1956.

Chorpenning, Charlotte B. *Rip Van Winkle.* (Children's Theatre Playscript Series). Morton Grove, Ill.: Coach House Press, Inc., 1954.

Ciardi, John. "On Flunking a Nice Boy Out of School" in *The Now Voices: Poetry of the Present.* Edited by Angelo Carli and Theodore Kilman. New York: Charles Scribner's Sons, 1971.

Clark, Walter van Tilburg. *The Ox-Bow Incident.* New York: New American Library, 1943.

Clifton, Lucille. "My Mama Moved Among the Days" in *Tangled Vines: A Collection of Mother and Daughter Poems.* Edited by Lyn Lifshin. Boston: Beacon Press, 1978.

Conrad, Joseph. *Heart of Darkness.* New York: Pocket Books, Inc., 1972.

Crane, Stephen. *The Red Badge of Courage.* New York: Bantam Books, Inc., 1981.

Crews, Donald. *Freight Train.* New York: Penguin Books, Inc., 1985.

Crews, Donald. *Harbor.* New York: Greenwillow Books, 1982.

Cunningham, Julia. *Dorp Dead.* New York: Avon Books, 1974.

Darwin, Charles. *The Descent of Man.* Philadelphia: Richard West, 1902.

De Angeli, Marguerite. *The Door in the Wall.* New York: Scholastic, Inc., 1984.

De Paola, Tomie. *The Cloud Book.* New York: Holiday House, Inc., 1984.

De Tocqueville, Alexis. *Democracy in America.* In two volumes. Edited by Phillips Bradley. New York: Random House, Inc., 1944.

The Diary of Anne Frank. Adapted by Linda A. Cadrain. West Haven, Conn.: Pendulum Press, Inc., 1979.

Dickens, Charles. *Oliver Twist.* New York: Bantam Books, Inc., 1981.

Dickens, Charles. *A Tale of Two Cities.* New York: Bantam Books, Inc., 1981.

Dumas, Alexandre. *The Count of Monte Cristo*. New York: Dodd, Mead & Co., 1984.

Eliot, T. S. *Old Possum's Book of Practical Cats*. San Diego, Calif.: Harcourt Brace Jovanovich, Inc., 1982.

Ellison, Ralph. *Invisible Man*. New York: Random House, Inc., 1972.

Estes, Eleanor. *The Hundred Dresses*. San Diego, Calif.: Harcourt Brace Jovanovich, Inc., 1974.

Ets, Marie H. *In the Forest*. New York: Penguin Books, Inc., 1976.

Farley, Walter. *The Black Stallion*. New York: Random House, Inc., 1982.

Fisher, Leonard E. *Star Signs*. New York: Holiday House, Inc., 1983.

Fitzgerald, F. Scott. "Diamond as Big as the Ritz" in *Six Tales of the Jazz Age and Other Stories*. New York: Charles Scribner's Sons, 1968.

Fitzhugh, Louise. *Harriet the Spy*. New York: Dell Publishing Co., Inc., 1984.

Flack, Marjorie. *Ask Mister Bear*. New York: Macmillan Publishing Co., Inc., 1932.

Forbes, Ester. *Johnny Tremain*. Cutchogue, N.Y.: Buccaneer Books, 1981.

Forester, C. S. *Captain Horatio Hornblower*. One volume edition. Boston: Little, Brown & Co., 1939.

The Fox and the Grapes (Aesop's Fables Book). Edited by Denise W. Guynn. Chicago: Society for Visual Education, Inc., 1980.

Fuentes, Carlos. *Cambio de piel* (Segunda edición). Guaymas, Mexico: Joaquin Mortiz, 1968.

Fuentes, Carlos. *A Change of Skin*. Translated by Sam Hileman. New York: Farrar, Straus and Giroux, 1986.

García Márquez, Gabriel. *Chronicle of a Death Foretold*. New York: Alfred A. Knopf, Inc., 1983.

García Márquez, Gabriel. *Crónica de una muerte anunciada*. Bogota: Editorial La Oveja Negra Ltda., 1981.

Gensler, Kinereth, and Nina Nyhart. *The Poetry Connection: An Anthology of Contemporary Poems with Ideas to Stimulate Children's Writing*. New York: Teachers and Writers Collaborative, 1978.

George, Jean C. *Julie of the Wolves*. New York: Harper & Row Junior Books, 1972.

Gibson, William. *The Miracle Worker*. New York: Alfred A. Knopf, Inc., 1957.

Gilson, Etienne. *Heloise and Abelard*. Ann Arbor, Mich.: University of Michigan Press, 1960.

Godden, Rumer. *The Mousewife*. New York: Viking-Penguin, Inc., 1982.

Goldilocks and the Three Bears. New York: Putnam Publishing Group, 1979.

Goodsell, Jane. *Eleanor Roosevelt*. New York: Thomas Y. Crowell Junior Books, 1970.

Grahame, Kenneth. *Wind in the Willows*. New York: New American Library, 1969.

Gray, Elizabeth J. *Adam of the Road*. New York: Viking-Penguin, Inc., 1942.

Greene, Constance C. *A Girl Called Al*. New York: Dell Publishing Co., Inc., 1977.

Haldane, J. B. *On Being the Right Size and Other Essays*. Edited by John M. Smith. New York: Oxford University Press, Inc., 1985.

Haley, Alex. *Roots*. Garden City, N.Y.: Doubleday & Co., Inc., 1976.

Haugaard, Erik C. *Leif the Unlucky*. Boston: Houghton Mifflin Co., 1982.

Hawthorne, Nathaniel. *The Scarlet Letter*. New York: Dodd, Mead & Co., 1984.

Hayden, Robert. "The Whipping" in *A Geography of Poets: An Anthology of the New Poetry*. Edited by Edward Field. New York: Bantam Books, Inc., 1979.

Henry, Marguerite. *Brighty of the Grand Canyon*. Chicago: Rand McNally & Co., 1953.

Henry, Marguerite. *King of the Wind*. Chicago: Rand McNally & Co., 1948.

Heyerdahl, Thor. *Kon-Tiki*. New York: Random House, Inc., 1984.

Holm, Anne. *North to Freedom*. Translated by L. W. Kingsland from Danish. San Diego, Calif.: Harcourt Brace Jovanovich, Inc., 1974.

Irving, Washington. *Rip Van Winkle*. North Pomfret, Vt.: David and Charles, 1982.

Jack and the Beanstalk. Mahwah, N.J.: Troll Assocs., 1979.

Joyce, James. *Dubliners*. New York: Penguin Books, Inc., 1976.

Juster, Norton. *The Phantom Tollbooth*. New York: Random House, Inc., 1961.

Kafka, Franz. *The Metamorphosis*. New York: Vanguard Pr., Inc., 1985.

Keller, Helen. *The Story of My Life*. Cutchogue, N.Y.: Buccaneer Books, 1984.

Kennedy, John F. *Profiles in Courage*. New York: Harper & Row Pubs., Inc., 1983.

King, Martin Luther, Jr. "I Have a Dream." Speech from *Makers of America,* Vol. 10. Edited by Wayne Moquin. Chicago: Encyclopaedia Britannica Educational Corp., 1971.

Kipling, Rudyard. *Kim*. New York: New American Library, 1984.

Koestler, Arthur. *Darkness at Noon*. New York: Macmillan Publishing Co., Inc., 1941.

Krauss, Ruth. *The Carrot Seed*. New York: Harper & Row Junior Books, 1945.

Lawrence, D. H. "The Rocking Horse Winner" in *The Oxford Book of Short Stories*. Edited by V. S. Pritchett. New York: Oxford University Press, Inc., 1981.

Leaf, Munro. *The Story of Ferdinand*. New York: Penguin Books, Inc., 1977.

Lee, Harper. *To Kill a Mockingbird*. New York: Harper & Row Pubs., Inc., 1961.

L'Engle, Madeleine. *A Wrinkle in Time*. New York: Dell Publishing Co., Inc., 1976.

London, Jack. *Call of the Wild*. New York: Macmillan Publishing Co., Inc., 1970.

Matthiessen, Peter. *Sal Si Puedes: Cesar Chavez and the New American Revolution*. New York: Random House, Inc., 1969.

Mayer, Mercer. *A Boy, a Dog, and a Frog*. New York: Dial Books for Young Readers, 1979.

Miller, Arthur. *Death of a Salesman*. New York: Penguin Books, Inc., 1976.

Milne, A. A. *When We Were Very Young*. New York: Dell Publishing Co., Inc., 1975.

Mosel, Arlene. *The Funny Little Woman*. New York: E. P. Dutton, 1977.

Nash, Ogden. *Parents Keep Out: Elderly Poems for Youngerly Readers*. Boston: Little, Brown & Co., 1951.

Neruda, Pablo. "Ode to a Fallen Chestnut" in *Selected Poems* (A Bilingual Edition). Edited by Nathaniel Tarn. New York: Dell Publishing Co., Inc., 1970.

Ness, Evaline. *Sam, Bangs and Moonshine*. New York: Holt, Rinehart & Winston, Inc., 1966.

O'Brien, Robert C. *Mrs. Frisby and the Rats of Nimh*. New York: Atheneum Pubs., 1971.

O'Dell, Scott. *Island of the Blue Dolphins*. New York: Dell Publishing Co., Inc., 1978.

Patterson, Lillie. *Frederick Douglass: Freedom Fighter*. Easton, Md.: Garrard Pub. Co., 1965.

Potter, Beatrix. *Peter Rabbit*. New York: Putnam Publishing Group, 1981.

Prokofiev, Sergei. *Peter and the Wolf*. Boston: David R. Godine Pub., Inc., 1980.

"The River-Merchant's Wife: A Letter." Translated from Chinese by Ezra Pound. In *The Harper Anthology of Poetry*. Edited by John Frederick Nims. New York: Harper & Row Pubs., Inc., 1981.

Rodgers, Mary. *Freaky Friday*. New York: Harper & Row Pubs., Inc., 1977.

Rodriguez, Richard. *Hunger of Memory: The Education of Richard Rodriguez, An Autobiography*. Boston: David R. Godine, Pub., Inc., 1981.

Rogers, Pamela. *The Rare One*. New York: Lodestar Books, 1974.

Ryan, Charles C. *The Starry Messenger: The Best of Galileo*. New York: St. Martin's Press, Inc., 1979.

Salten, Felix. *Bambi*. Cutchogue, N.Y.: Buccaneer Books, 1981.

Sandburg, Carl. *Abe Lincoln Grows Up*. San Diego, Calif.: Harcourt Brace Jovanovich, Inc., 1975.

Schaefer, Jack. *Shane*. New York: Bantam Books, Inc., 1980.

Sendak, Maurice. *Where the Wild Things Are*. New York: Harper & Row Junior Books, 1963.

Shakespeare, William. *Hamlet*. Edited by T. J. Spencer. New York: Penguin Books, Inc., 1981.

Shakespeare, William. *Romeo and Juliet*. New York: Alfred A. Knopf, Inc., 1983.

Shakespeare, William. Sonnet 130, "My Mistress' Eyes Are Nothing Like the Sun" in *Beginnings in Poetry*. Edited by William J. Matz. Glenview, Ill.: Scott Foresman & Co., 1973.

Shulman, Irving. *West Side Story*. New York: Pocket Books, Inc., 1961.

Singer, Isaac Bashevis. *A Day of Pleasure: Stories of a Boy Growing up in Warsaw*. New York: Farrar, Straus & Giroux, Inc., 1969.

Smart, Christopher. *For I Will Consider My Cat Jeoffry*. New York: Atheneum Pubs., 1984.

Sone, Monica. *Nisei Daughter*. Seattle, Wash.: University of Washington Press, 1979.

Sophocles. *Oedipus Rex*. Edited by R. D. Dawe. New York: Cambridge University Press, 1982.

Spier, Peter. *People*. New York: Doubleday & Co., Inc., 1980.

Stafford, William. "Fifteen" in *Sounds and Silences: Poetry for Now*. Edited by Richard Peck. New York: Dell Publishing Co., Inc., 1970.

Stevens, Janet. *The Tortoise and the Hare: An Aesop Fable*. New York: Holiday House, Inc., 1984.

Stevenson, Robert Louis. *Kidnapped*. New York: New American Library, 1959.

Stevenson, Robert Louis. *The Strange Case of Dr. Jekyll and Mr. Hyde*. Edited by Raymond Harris. Providence, R.I.: Jamestown Pubs., Inc., 1982.

"Sweet William's Ghost" in *As I Walked Out One Evening: A Book of Ballads*. Compiled by Helen Plotz. New York: Greenwillow Books, 1976.

Swift, Jonathan. *Gulliver's Travels*. New York: Oxford University Press, 1977.

Switzer, Ellen. *The Nutcracker: A Story and a Ballet.* New York: Atheneum Pubs., 1985.

Taylor, Mildred. *Roll of Thunder, Hear My Cry.* New York: Bantam Books, Inc., 1978.

Thomas, Lewis. *The Lives of a Cell: Notes of a Biology Watcher.* New York: Penguin Books, Inc., 1978.

Thoreau, Henry David. *Civil Disobedience.* Edited by Edmund R. Brown. Brookline Village, Mass.: Branden Publishing Co., n.d.

The Three Billy Goats Gruff. Edited by Marcia Brown. San Diego, Calif.: Harcourt Brace Jovanovich, Inc., 1957.

Turkle, Brinton. *Deep in the Forest.* New York: E. P. Dutton, 1976.

Twain, Mark. *The Adventures of Huckleberry Finn.* New York: New American Library, 1971.

Twain, Mark. *The Adventures of Tom Sawyer.* New York: New American Library, 1959.

Uchida, Yoshiko. *Samurai of Gold Hill* (Revised edition). Berkeley, Calif.: Creative Arts Book. Co., 1985.

Viorst, Judith. *Alexander and the Terrible, Horrible, No Good, Very Bad Day.* New York: Atheneum Pubs., 1972.

Viorst, Judith. *The Tenth Good Thing About Barney.* New York: Atheneum Pubs., 1975.

Waber, Bernard. *Ira Sleeps Over.* Boston: Houghton Mifflin Co., 1975.

West, Jessamyn. *Massacre at Fall Creek.* San Diego, Calif.: Harcourt Brace Jovanovich, 1975.

White, E. B. *Charlotte's Web.* New York: Harper & Row Junior Books, 1952.

Wilder, Laura I. *Little House Books.* In nine volumes. New York: Harper & Row Junior Books, 1973.

Wilder, Thornton. *Our Town.* New York: Avon Books, 1975.

Wildsmith, Brian. *Circus.* New York: Oxford University Press, Inc., 1970.

Williams, Tennessee. *The Glass Menagerie.* New York: New Directions Publishing Corp., n.d.

Wister, Owen. *The Virginian.* New York: New American Library, 1983.

Wordsworth, William. Sonnet, "Composed Upon Westminster Bridge, 3 September, 1802" in *Beginnings in Poetry.* Edited by William J. Martz. Glenview, Ill.: Scott, Foresman & Co., 1973.

Wright, Richard. *Black Boy: A Record of Childhood and Youth.* New York: Harper & Row Pubs., Inc., 1969.

Yashima, Taro. *Crow Boy.* New York: Penguin Books, Inc., 1976.

Other Sources

"Library Bill of Rights" (Revised edition). Chicago: Office of Intellectual Freedom, American Library Association, 1980.

The Students' Right to Read. Champaign, Ill.: Committee on the Right to Read of the National Council of Teachers of English, 1962. (brochure).

Publications Available from the Department of Education

This publication is one of over 650 that are available from the California Department of Education. Some of the more recent publications or those most widely used are the following:

ISBN	Title (Date of publication)	Price
0-8011-0271-5	Academic Honesty (1986)	$2.50
0-8011-0722-9	Accounting Procedures for Student Organizations (1988)	3.75
0-8011-0272-3	Administration of Maintenance and Operations in California School Districts (1986)	6.75
0-8011-0275-8	California Dropouts: A Status Report (1986)	2.50
0-8011-0862-4	California Education Summit: Final Report and Background Papers (2 Vols.) (1990)	5.00
0-8011-0783-0	California Private School Directory, 1988-89 (1988)	14.00
0-8011-0853-5	California Public School Directory (1990)	14.00
0-8011-0488-2	Caught in the Middle: Educational Reform for Young Adolescents in California Public Schools (1987)	5.00
0-8011-0777-6	The Changing Mathematics Curriculum: A Booklet for Parents (1989)	10 for 5.00*
0-8011-0241-3	Computer Applications Planning (1985)	5.00
0-8011-0833-0	Directory of Microcomputer Software for School Business Administration (1990)	7.50
0-8011-0818-7	Dreams of Flying (videocassette) (1989)	30.00
0-8011-0749-0	Educational Software Preview Guide, 1988-89 (1988)	2.00
0-8011-0489-0	Effective Practices in Achieving Compensatory Education-Funded Schools II (1987)	5.00
0-8011-0041-0	English–Language Arts Framework for California Public Schools (1987)	3.00
0-8011-0731-8	English–Language Arts Model Curriculum Guide, K—8 (1988)	3.00
0-8011-0710-5	Family Life/Sex Education Guidelines (1987)	4.00
0-8011-0289-8	Handbook for Physical Education (1986)	4.50
0-8011-0249-9	Handbook for Planning an Effective Foreign Language Program (1985)	3.50
0-8011-0320-7	Handbook for Planning an Effective Literature Program (1987)	3.00
0-8011-0290-1	Handbook for Planning an Effective Writing Program (1986)	2.50
0-8011-0680-x	Handbook for Teaching Japanese-Speaking Students (1987)	4.50
0-8011-0291-x	Handbook for Teaching Pilipino-Speaking Students (1986)	4.50
0-8011-0250-2	Handbook on California Education for Language Minority Parents—Chinese/English Edition (1985)†	3.25
0-8011-0712-1	History–Social Science Framework for California Public Schools (1988)	6.00
0-8011-0782-2	Images: A Workbook for Enhancing Self-esteem and Promoting Career Preparation, Especially for Black Girls (1988)	6.00
0-8011-0877-2	Infant/Toddler Caregiving: A Guide to Routines (1990)	8.25
0-8011-0828-4	Instructor's Behind-the-Wheel Guide for California's Bus Driver's Training Course (1989)	20.00
0-8011-0358-4	Mathematics Framework for California Public Schools (1985)	3.00
0-8011-0664-8	Mathematics Model Curriculum Guide, K—8 (1987)	2.75
0-8011-0725-3	Model Curriculum for Human Rights and Genocide (1988)	3.25

*Also available in quantities of 100 for $30.00 and 1,000 for $230.00.

†The following editions are also available, at the same price: Armenian/English, Cambodian/English, Hmong/English, Japanese/English, Korean/English, Laotian/English, Pilipino/English, Spanish/English, and Vietnamese/English.

*Appendixes to this report are also available.

Orders should be directed to:

California Department of Education
P.O. Box 271
Sacramento, CA 95802-0271

Please include the International Standard Book Number (ISBN) for each title ordered.

Remittance or purchase order must accompany order. Purchase orders without checks are accepted only from governmental agencies. Sales tax should be added to all orders from California purchasers.

A complete list of publications available from the Department, including apprenticeship instructional materials, may be obtained by writing to the address listed above or by calling (916) 445-1260.

90 81137

F90-33 (Third printing) 913-0005 300 7-90 12M

ENGLISH 9th GRADE

COURSE DESCRIPTION: 9th grade English will consist of a literature-based curriculum with a strong writing component. The course will emphasis the integrattion of reading, writing , speaking and listening skills. The students will study various forms of literature, such as the novel, the short story, drama, poetry and the essay. Interpretation of literature will grow from the understanding of a concept or a theme. The student will consider literature and writing as reflection, opportunities for encouraging self-growth' and self-esteem.

PERFORMANCE OBJECTIVES: A)Students will become acquainted with the sturctures of various genres: the novel, the short story, drama, poetry and the essay.

B) Students will become acquainted with universal mythologics, both Western and Eastern. Included is the study of the pattern of the hero's journey.

C) Students will be introduced to the elements of literature: characterization, setting, plot, theme and the author's point of view.

D. Students will be able to write a cohesive paragraph with a clear topic sentence and supportive details.

E. Students will learn the Autobiographical Incident and Observational Writing modes.

F. Students will learn language skills basic to clear and effective speaking and listening.

G. Students will learn vocabulary as an integral part of the classroom curriculum.

H. Students will be introduced to the use of the library.

ENGLISH 10th GRADE

COURSE DESCRIPTION: Tenth grade English will consist of a literature-based curriculum with a strong writing component, building on the 9th grade curriculum. (see ENGLISH 9th grade)

PERFORMANCE OBJECTIVES:

A) Students will apply the elements of fiction to their understanding of literature.

B) Students will apply the concept of universal myth to the understanding of literature.

C) Students will learn the expository essya structure.

D) Students will learn Report of Information (I-Search) and Biographical Sketch as modes of writing.

E) Students will learn vocabulary as an integral part of the curriculum.

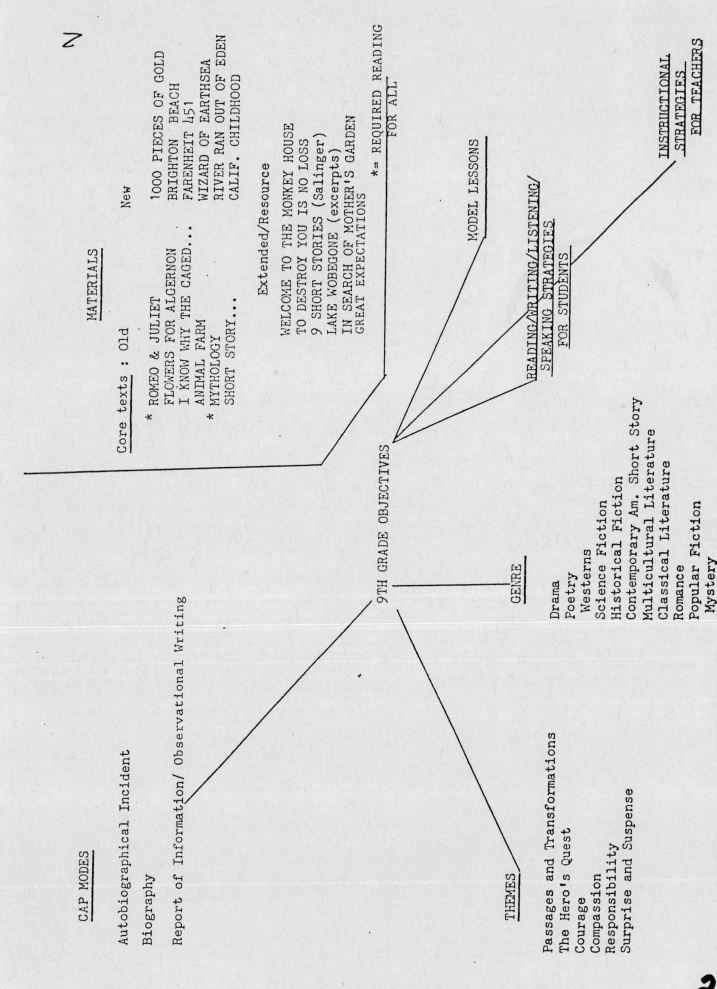

CAP MODES

Autobiographical Incident

Biography

Report of Information/ Observational Writing

MATERIALS

Core texts : Old   New

* ROMEO & JULIET   1000 PIECES OF GOLD
FLOWERS FOR ALGERNON   BRIGHTON BEACH
I KNOW WHY THE CAGED...   FARENHEIT 451
ANIMAL FARM   WIZARD OF EARTHSEA
* MYTHOLOGY   RIVER RAN OUT OF EDEN
SHORT STORY....   CALIF. CHILDHOOD

Extended/Resource

WELCOME TO THE MONKEY HOUSE
TO DESTROY YOU IS NO LOSS
9 SHORT STORIES (Salinger)
LAKE WOBEGONE (excerpts)
IN SEARCH OF MOTHER'S GARDEN
GREAT EXPECTATIONS

* = REQUIRED READING
FOR ALL

9TH GRADE OBJECTIVES

MODEL LESSONS

READING/WRITING/LISTENING/
SPEAKING STRATEGIES
FOR STUDENTS

INSTRUCTIONAL
STRATEGIES
FOR TEACHERS

GENRE

Drama
Poetry
Westerns
Science Fiction
Historical Fiction
Contemporary Am. Short Story
Multicultural Literature
Classical Literature
Romance
Popular Fiction
Mystery

THEMES

Passages and Transformations
The Hero's Quest
Courage
Compassion
Responsibility
Surprise and Suspense

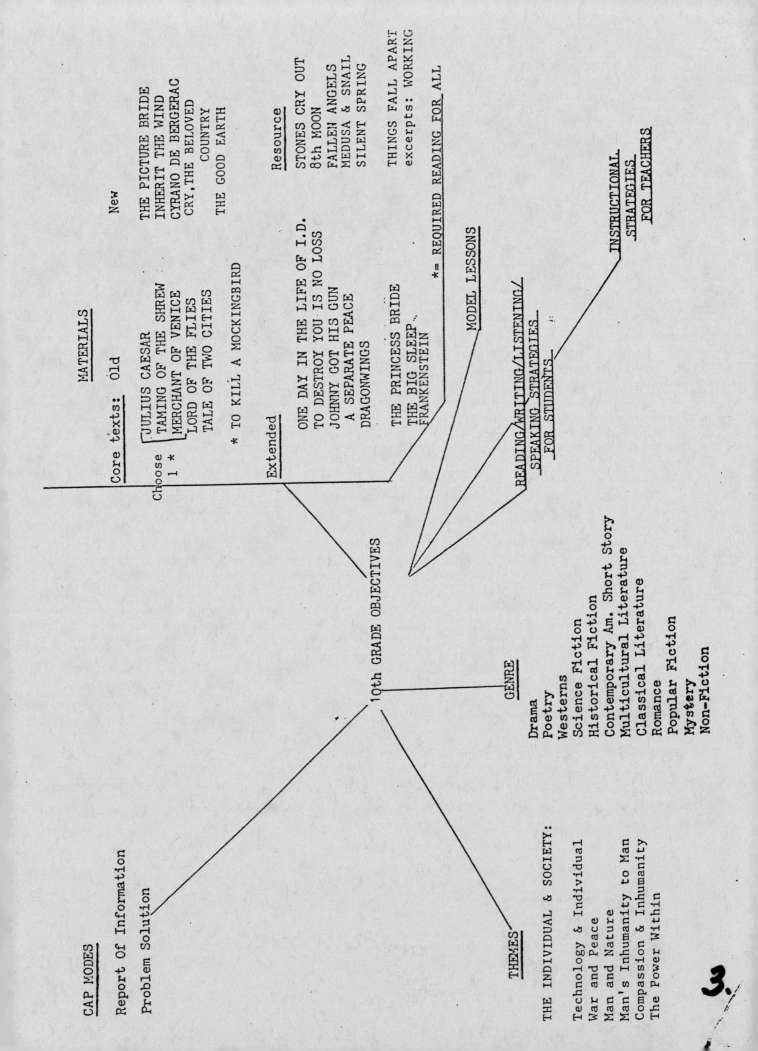

CAP MODES

Report Of Information
Problem Solution

MATERIALS

Core texts: Old   New

Choose 1 *

Old	New
JULIUS CAESAR	THE PICTURE BRIDE
TAMING OF THE SHREW	INHERIT THE WIND
MERCHANT OF VENICE	CYRANO DE BERGERAC
LORD OF THE FLIES	CRY, THE BELOVED COUNTRY
TALE OF TWO CITIES	THE GOOD EARTH

* TO KILL A MOCKINGBIRD

Extended	Resource
ONE DAY IN THE LIFE OF I.D.	STONES CRY OUT
TO DESTROY YOU IS NO LOSS	8th MOON
JOHNNY GOT HIS GUN	FALLEN ANGELS
A SEPARATE PEACE	MEDUSA & SNAIL
DRAGONWINGS	SILENT SPRING
THE PRINCESS BRIDE	THINGS FALL APART
THE BIG SLEEP	excerpts: WORKING
FRANKENSTEIN	

*= REQUIRED READING FOR ALL

MODEL LESSONS

READING/WRITING/LISTENING/
SPEAKING STRATEGIES
FOR STUDENTS

INSTRUCTIONAL
STRATEGIES
FOR TEACHERS

10th GRADE OBJECTIVES

GENRE

Drama
Poetry
Westerns
Science Fiction
Historical Fiction
Contemporary Am. Short Story
Multicultural Literature
Classical Literature
Romance
Popular Fiction
Mystery
Non-Fiction

THEMES

THE INDIVIDUAL & SOCIETY:

Technology & Individual
War and Peace
Man and Nature
Man's Inhumanity to Man
Compassion & Inhumanity
The Power Within

3.

COMPREHENSIVE ENGLISH

English 9 and 10 (so far)

EDUCATIONAL PHILOSOPHY

Students are the focus of all endeavors of these courses. Educating the student- academically, socially, emotionally and ethically- within the boundaries of district guidelines is the primary goal. The teacher as a positive role model provides students with the opportunities, expectations and encouragement to grow and excel. Growth requires risk-taking and experimentation since the quality of experiences is often as important to the outcomes. The classroom environment should foster a personal responsibility for self, others and the world community. The classroom provides a flexible structure that facilitates active learning for all. Students are given opportunities to engage in and own the decision-making process. They need to explore personal interests. Students are trained to work as teams, leading to self-esteem and respect for cultural diversity.

GOALS AND OBJECTIVES

The goals and objectives for all 9th and 10th graders are the same. See the chart which describes each course and its performance objectives.

THEMES/ CAP MODES/ MATERIALS

The themes/ required CAP modes/ materials for both 9th and 10th graders are outlined on the maps corresponding to each course.

FOCUSED TRAINING FOR ENGLISH 9

1. Students will learn strategies and behavior that help them participate effectively in cooperative group learning..
Students will learn the following skills:

    - checks others' understanding of the work
    - contributes ideas, information, opinions
    - stays on task and gets group back to work
    - paraphrases
    - seeks information and opinions
    - follows directions
    - organizes working conditions for maximum productivity
    - encourages and praises
    - acknowledges contributions
    - maintains eye contact and actively listens
    - expresses appreciation
    - shares feelings

- disagrees in an agreeable way
- resolves conflict
- criticizes ideas, not people
- actively participates
- assumes responsibility for roles

*RESOURCE FOR INSTRUCTIONAL STRATEGIES
     -(pink spiral notebook thingy)
     - Designing Groupwork (E. Cohen)

2. Students will learn fluency in writing.

   *RESOURCES FOR INSTRUCTIONAL STRATEGIES
        - Active Voices (Moffett's levels of thinking)

3. Students will be familiar with all steps in the writing
process: prewriting, precomposing, drafting,
responding/revising,editing,publication, evaluation and
feedback.

   *RESOURCES
        -Cooper Guides
        -CAP Writing Guides
        -Sharing Writing

4. Students will be able to demonstrate the following skills
in writing: 1) select and narrow topics for writing, 2)
supply appropriate and significant information, 3) organize
and present content to meet reader's needs, 4) modulate
voice depending on audience and purpose, and 5)follow the
customs of spelling, mechanics, usage and legibility.

5. Students will derive an appreciation for reading by
discovering meaning from the text. The student will practice
the following skills:

   - development of good reading habits
   - selection of novels that interest student
   - evaluation and sharing of reading material
   - predictions based on context
   - vocabulary development through context clues
   - identification of conflict where students propose
     practical solutions for its resolutions
   - understanding of character motivation/actions
   - summary and paraphrase of plot
   - speculation about outcomes
   - use of library as a resource to locate books, infor-
     mation and materials related to a theme or topic
   - interpretation of character, theme, events and
     selected passages.

*RESOURCES
        -Sustained Silent Reading daily
        -Dr. Fraim's Reading Journal packet
        -(graphic organizers material)
        -Language, Literacy and Learning (Langer, Mog)
        -Literature for All Students: A Sourcebook for
            Teachers (Cal Literature Institute,1985)

FOCUSED TRAINING FOR ENGLISH 10

1. Students will continue training in the cooperative
strategies list under English 9.

2. Students ill focus on precomposing (graphic organizers)
and revision strategies in the writing process.

        *RESOURCES
            -Sharing Writing

3. Students will learn to develop an expository paragraph
which includes logic and support (topic sentence/claim,
explanatory sentence/link, supportive detail/evidence).

        *RESOURCE
            - Perfect Paragraph filmstrip
            - CAP Writing Guide for Interpretation

4. Students will learn to interpret a thematic statement by
analyzing character, plot and conflict; specifically in a
novel or novelette.

EVALUATION: 1) Portfolio
              2) CAP Scoring Guides
              3) Student evaluation

Other ideas that need exploration...

    We felt the the Gates Reading Test was not sufficient in
assessing student reading comprehension. The items had
nothing to do with the learning in the classroom. We suggest
an exploration of a more authentic reflection of student
performance. Could we get a group together to look into
developing a better tool for our department in assessment of
students for placement?

    We also thought that it would be resourceful to compile
a list of titles for short stories, poems, articles, etc. on
a particular subject or theme that a student could call up
when moving through these units. How could we orchestrate
this?

6

TO: ALL TEACHERS OF SOPHOMORES

RE: STANDARDS FOR SOPHOMORE PERFORMANCE

ENGLISH 10 HONORS

1. ABILITY

    * Reading: +12.0 (Gates)
    * Grades: Maintains an A or B in a 9 Honors with no
struggle
            Maintains an A in 9CP with no struggle
    * Clear thinking and writing skills
    * Clear verbal expression
    * Genuine interest in English
    * Teacher recommendation

2. COURSE EXPECTATIONS

    * to complete nightly homework (equal to 2 classes?)
    * to write fluently and proficiently in both narrative
and expository modes
    * to read both assigned and extended reading

3. GOALS

    * to enter a four-year university

ENGLISH 10CP

1. ABILITY

    * Reading +9.0
    * should be able to maintain a C in 9CP with no
struggle

2. COURSE EXPECTATIONS

    * to complete nightly homework
    * to be fluent in writing
    * to know the steps in the writing process
    * to demonstrate knowledge of form and correctness
commensurate with grade level (e.g. topic sentence,
movement of a developmental paragraph, evidence).
    * to read both assigned and extended reading

3. GOALS

    * to enter a 4 year university

7

ENGLISH 10   (Comprehensive English)

1. ABILITY

    * Reading -9.0
    * Working to achieve grade level in both reading and
       writing skills

2. EXPECTATIONS

    * to be motivated enough to work on critical reading
       skills
    * to learn to write fluently
    * to learn to write a developmental paragraph

3. GOAL

    * to achieve grade level reading and writing skills
    * to pass District competencies in reading and
composition

8

MATERIALS

The following titles and units were suggested:

1930's

Grapes of Wrath - Steinbeck
All the Kings Men
No Promises in the Wind
Their Eyes Were Watching God, Thurston
Tortilla Flat
Native Son, Richard Wright
Films/Videos - "American Me" and Lemon Grove

1940's

The Color Purple - Walker
The Invisible Man, Ellison
"The Chicken that Became a Rat"
"The Wave" - WW II Video
War Lover - Hersey
Over the River and Through the Woods
Battle Hymn
Winds of War - Wouk
Rumors of Peace - Ella Leflan
The Human Comedy - Wm. Saroyan

1950's

Catcher in the Rye
A Raisin in the Sun, Hansberr

1860-1890 - Westward Expansion

Men to Match my Mountains - Irving Stone
Journals - American Women Moving West
The Wilderness Reader, edited by Frank Bergon
The Road for Coorain, Jill Ker Conway
Ordeal by Hunger (The Donner Party)
Bury my Heart at Wound Knee
Beloved, Toni Morrison
Westering Man, Biography of Joseph Walker
Women's Pioneer Journals
American Indian Anthology - Wayne
The Adventures of Huckleberry Finn - Twain

1891-1916 - World War One

Johnny Get Your Gun
Pads of Glory
Winesburg Ohio, Sherwood Anderson
Editha, Howell, W.D.
Autobiography of an Ex-colored Man, James Johnson

1920's

The Great Gatsby - Fitzgerad
Babbit - Sinclair Lewis
Main Street
Harlem Renaissance poetry - Langston Hughes/Claude McKay
Inherit the Wind

CORE TEXTS

The Great Gatsby
Huckleberry Finn
Raisin in the Sun or Death of a Salesman

MODEL LESSONS

Reading, Writing, Listening, Speaking Strategies for Students
Instructional Strategies for Teachers

11th Grade Objectives

CAP MODES

Interpretation
Reflection

THEMES

Westward Expansion and the Immigrant Experience
Idealism and Disillusionment (WW I)
Success and Excess (1920s)
The American Dream Unraveled (1930s)
WW II
Conformity and the Illusion of Prosperity (1950s)
Civil Rights and Wrongs

9

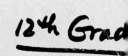

MATERIALS

Old

*HAMLET (Shakespeare) (See note)
*JANE EYRE (Brontë)
1984 (Orwell)
THINGS FALL APART (Achebe)
LES MISERABLES (Hugo)
CYRANO DE BERGERAC (Rostand)
OEDIPUS REX (trilogy) (Sophocles)
ANTIGONE (Sophocles)
THE ODYSSEY (Homer)
OTHELLO (Shakespeare)
THE IMPORTANCE OF
   BEING EARNEST (Wilde)

"The Second Coming" (Yeats)
"The Lovesong of J.
   Alfred Prufrock" (Eliot)
"The Lady of Shallot"
"My Last Duchess" (Browning)

New

Extended

KAFFIR BOY (Mathabane)
ORDINARY PEOPLE (Guest)
THE GOOD CONSCIENCE (Fuentes)
ANNA KARENINA (Tolstoy)
MADAME BOVARY (Flaubert)
NIGHT (Wiesel)
ISHI: THE LAST OF HIS TRIBE
SPIDER WOMAN'S GRANDAUGHTERS
CONTEMPORARY READER (Eng. 12)
LORD OF THE FLIES (Eng. 12)
PRINCE OF TIDES (Conroy)
short stories by Nadine
   Gordimer & Bessie Head (S.Af.)
Pamphlets: Controversial Issues
Woman Warrior (Hong Kingston)

RESOURCES FOR TEACHER STRATEGIES

LANGUAGE, LITERACY AND LEARNING
   Connections (Langer & Mog)

STRATEGIES FOR STUDENTS

Choice of Interpretive Frameworks from
   student repertoire
Research-based group work
Demonstration of understanding through
   portfolio (includes performance)

CAP MODES

Controversial Issue

Speculation About Cause/Effect

RESOURCES: CAP Writing Guides
   Cooper Guides

12th GRADE
PERFORMANCE OBJECTIVES

*Alienation/Fragmentation
*Family units (Love/dysfunction)
*Social Responsibilities (Justice)
* Dignity as source of strength
   (self-respect/harmony)

THEMES

POWER

the struggle to discover the nature
of power within the self, within
relationships and within society.
An examination of issues evolving from
one's responsibilities, the confrontation
with "the dark side" of the power struggle.
struggle. Contracts of power (win/lose,
lose/lose, win/win) and the sense
of powerlessness explored through
the following subthemes.

PREREQUISITES FOR PLACEMENT IN HONORS/ AP COURSES

1. ACADEMIC ACHIEVEMENT

Students who are eligible for placement in the Honors/AP program are high achievers in academics. These students have maintained appropriate study habits that are required to keep pace with a rigorous course of reading and composition. Nightly homework is routine and students are expected to be prepared for class lessons following each homework assignment. Students should expect homework on most weekends. The Honor students will be trained in higher level thinking skills that will become important strategies for critical readign and writing about literature.

A student who is eligible for the Honors program needs to maintain an A or a B in a college preparatory course or in an Honors course. Or, the student must maintain an A or a B in his 8th grade English course.

2. MOTIVATION AND GENERAL LOVE FOR ENGLISH

The Honors student must have a genuine interest in the study of literature and of writing. Since the course is rigorous and is aimed at challenging those who are academically proficient, an Honor student is an avid reader. In addition, he uses writing as a process for discovery and enjoyment.

The Honor student will be motivated to do well not solely for the grade, but for the satisfaction he gets from discovery about the meaning of literature and the concepts inherent in the course content.

3. ASSESSMENT STANDARDS

Honor students must read at or above the following levels as measured by the Gates-McGinitie Reading Test:

9th grade- +10.5
10th grade- +11.0
11th grade- +12.0

In addition, the student's teacher will score a writing sample based on an interpretive prompt to judge eligibility for the Honors program.

4. TEACHER AND DEPARTMENT HEAD APPROVAL

The Honor student must have his English teacher's recommendation and the approval of the Department Chairman. Because of limited space, Honors courses will be offered as one class per track for both 9th and 10th grades. 11th grade Honors will be offered only on A and C tracks, one section per track. Likewise, AP will be offered only on A and C tracks. Class size is limited to 30 students.